W9-AUZ-871

"David Anderson speaks, lives and is called to the truth of multicultural relationships and ministry. This book is not a book just for black people to work with whites or whites to learn how to be sensitive to blacks, but a book about God's practical, real transforming grace for all people to be kingdom people."

PHIL JACKSON, LEAD PASTOR, THE HOUSE, AND COAUTHOR OF *THE HIP-HOP CHURCH*

"David Anderson addresses one of the real solutions to the issue of racism with this difficult practice of grace! David's take from an African American perspective enlightens us to how deep racism runs even in Christian institutions and relationships, but more than that, he also offers us a biblical initiative to lead us to the vision of being a community that reflects the diversity of God."

DAVE GIBBONS, LEAD PASTOR, NEWSONG CHURCH, AND CVO, XEALOT INC.

"With profound concepts and a compelling voice, *Gracism* creates an accessible tool for navigating culture clashes. Anderson merges a sophisticated understanding of cultural dynamics with real-time, everyday advice. He takes old-time concepts like 'favor' and gives them flesh and blood for a modern world."

NIKKI A. TOYAMA, COEDITOR OF *MORE THAN SERVING TEA: ASIAN AMERICAN WOMEN ON EXPECTATIONS, RELATIONSHIPS, LEADERSHIP AND FAITH*

"David Anderson is a powerful voice of hope and a national leader in racial reconciliation. This book provides a new—and the only—'ism' that can heal the deep wounds of racism."

DONALD T. FLOYD JR., PRESIDENT AND CEO, NATIONAL 4-H COUNCIL

"Anderson provides us with more than just a theoretical or political rationale for Christians to work toward racial reconciliation. He also provides us with practical methods by which this reconciliation may be achieved. *Gracism* needs to become a term common to Christians of all races. As we follow the advice in this important book we will find ourselves becoming inclusive of those who are different than us. As Anderson so ably demonstrates, it is when we develop the heart and skills necessary for such a conclusion that we will be able to truly adopt Christlike attitudes toward our racially different neighbors and colleagues."

GEORGE YANCEY, ASSOCIATE PROFESSOR OF SOCIOLOGY, UNIVERSITY OF NORTH TEXAS, AND AUTHOR OF *BEYOND RACIAL GRIDLOCK* AND *ONE BODY, ONE SPIRIT*

"After reading this book, I am convinced: we need gracism. Division and inequality are consequences of our fallen world. But as the members of the church we must walk against division and injustice. The brilliance of this book is that we are shown how to overcome individual-level racism, clearly and plainly. Dr. Anderson provides us with real tools for real life. Gracism is an act, a state of being. Members of the body, let's be gracists."

MICHAEL EMERSON, FOUNDING DIRECTOR, CENTER ON RACE, RELIGION, AND URBAN LIFE, RICE UNIVERSITY, AND COAUTHOR OF *DIVIDED BY FAITH* AND *UNITED BY FAITH*

"Dr. David Anderson has given us both a great new word and a fresh way to approach our racial and cultural divisions in the church—and in life. I'm hoping a huge audience will read this book and discover the heart and passion of one of the racial reconciliation movement's most dynamic young leaders."

EDWARD GILBREATH, AUTHOR OF *RECONCILIATION BLUES: A BLACK EVANGELICAL'S INSIDE VIEW OF WHITE CHRISTIANITY*

"A tough-minded book and clear-sighted look at what it means for Christians to 'overcome evil with good.' If metaphor is metamorphosis, the metaphor of 'gracism' will change how we do church like it's changed how I do life."

LEONARD SWEET, AUTHOR OF *THE GOSPEL ACCORDING TO STARBUCKS,* AND E. STANLEY JONES PROFESSOR OF EVANGELISM, DREW THEOLOGICAL SCHOOL

"Dr. David Anderson is one of the finest reconciliation practitioners that I know. In this book, *Gracism: The Art of Inclusion,* he honestly shares his journey into a profound concept that has the potential to revolutionize how we confront racism to create a society with liberty and justice for all."

BRENDA SALTER MCNEIL, PRESIDENT AND FOUNDER, SALTER MCNEIL & ASSOCIATES, AND COAUTHOR OF *THE HEART OF RACIAL JUSTICE*

"What a beautiful—and needed!—book. Dave Anderson calls people who are saved by the grace of God to extend grace to their neighbors, whoever they are. I can't imagine anyone reading this book without being marked for life as an agent of gracism, which may be the best synonym for *reconciliation* ever invented."

BRIAN D. MCLAREN, AUTHOR/ACTIVIST

GRACISM

The Art of Inclusion

David A. Anderson

IVP Books

An imprint of InterVarsity Press
Downers Grove, Illinois

InterVarsity Press
P.O. Box 1400, Downers Grove, IL 60515-1426
World Wide Web: www.ivpress.com
E-mail: email@ivpress.com

InterVarsity Press® is the book-publishing division of InterVarsity Christian Fellowship/USA®, a student movement active on campus at hundreds of universities, colleges and schools of nursing in the United States of America, and a member movement of the International Fellowship of Evangelical Students. For information about local and regional activities, write Public Relations Dept., InterVarsity Christian Fellowship/USA, 6400 Schroeder Rd., P.O. Box 7895, Madison, WI 53707-7895, or visit the IVCF website at <www.intervarsity.org>.

Design: Cindy Kiple

Images: Nikki Ward/istockphoto.com

ISBN 978-0-8308-3440-2

Printed in Canada ∞

Library of Congress Cataloging-in-Publication Data

Anderson, David A., 1966-
Gracism: the art of inclusion / David A. Anderson.
  p. cm.
Includes bibliographical references.
ISBN 978-0-8308-3440-2 (cloth: alk. paper)
1. Church and minorities. 2. Social integration—Religious
aspects—Christianity. 3. Multiculturalism—Religious
aspects—Christianity. 4. Marginality, Social—Religious
aspects—Christianity. 5. Christianity and culture. 6.
Reconciliation—Religious aspects—Christianity. I. Title.
  BV639.M56A53 2007
  241'.675—dc22

                                                              2007011178

P	18	17	16	15	14	13	12	11	10	9	8	7	6	5	4	3	2	1
Y	22	21	20	19	18	17	16	15	14	13	12	11	10	09	08	07

CONTENTS

INTRODUCTION

Excited about my opportunity to serve as an intern at Willow Creek Community Church in South Barrington, Illinois, I was looking forward to my first day on the job. After three years of Bible education in downtown Chicago at Moody Bible Institute, and two years of urban pastoral ministry in Cabrini Green, a poor black neighborhood replete with high-rise apartments fencing in humans like rats in a cage, I was now about to enter a completely different experience.

As a tall African American male, my new reality as a Willow employee placed me in a suburban context among a sea of white people. This context included beautifully designed mansions and shiny luxury vehicles that occupied multiple garages. The landscaped lawns were works of art religiously primped and usually cared for by Hispanic men who edged and mowed the well-manicured acreage. It was a far cry from the urine-stained elevators and graffiti-ridden projects of Cabrini.

I wasn't raised in either extreme. I didn't come from wealth or poverty. Both of my parents worked full-time jobs outside the home but made it home each night by dinner time, when we all ate together. Our single-family home was a small brick Cape Cod with three bedrooms, one bathroom, a basement and a yard surrounded by a chain-link fence. My father worked for the federal government, while my mother worked for the state of Maryland. We four children attended public schools. During my elementary school years, I stayed with a neighborhood day-care provider after school until Mom came home from work.

Heading to Chicago was a big deal for me because I had seldom traveled beyond the Washington metropolitan area. My home metropolis was demographically diverse and there everyone seemed to work hard to hold down their jobs, pay their mortgages and protect their families from the social ills of drugs and violence. Once I landed in Chicago, though, the extremes of racial existence were stark. It seemed as if the majority of whites were rich and educated, while the blacks were poor and uneducated. The Hispanics were in their own enclaves and the Asians were seemingly invisible except in Chinatown or Korea town. For me as a minister in my twenties, my views about diversity, class distinctions, social conditioning and racial reconciliation were challenging my vision for multicultural ministry amid the extremes of society.

While I had grown up conscious of race and the differences that plagued our country both personally and systemically, I had never felt as powerless as I did on my first day as an intern at Willow. The day was marked by a racially penetrating event that is etched in my memory. As I commuted to the church that first morning in a rusted-out blue Honda Civic, I noticed blue lights flashing in my rear-view mirror. A police officer was signaling me to pull over. With my hands in clear view, I gave the officer my license and registration. He went back to his vehicle. I assumed he was checking my information on the computer and doing whatever else police officers do in their cars while the stopped driver sits in embarrassment along the side of the road as motorists pass and gawk.

When the officer returned to my driver's side window, he handed my license to me. I was dismissed.

"Before you leave, sir, can you tell me why I was pulled over?" I asked.

The officer responded, "You fit the description of someone we are looking for."

I took him at his word.

Had that been my only experience of being pulled over that day, I would have believed that the inconvenience of mistaken identity could have happened to anyone. But a few hours later I drove off the church campus to get lunch. Again I had the sinking feeling in my stomach that comes with the realization that one is being stopped by a police officer.

"What's wrong now?" I said aloud to myself. *Bad luck indeed,* I thought.

Like it was déjà vu, I went through the same delay that made me late on my first day of work earlier that morning. I received from the second officer the same explanation given to me by the first cop who had stopped me. "You fit the description of someone we are looking for," he said. At this point I thought it would be great if the officers could make a note in their system to let everyone know that David Anderson was not the guy they were looking for! I was upset.

What made the day so memorable was not the orientation to one of the coolest megachurches I had been exposed to at the time or the grace with which the staff greeted me when I was introduced. What was most memorable was that I was tardy on my first day as an intern due to a delay from a police officer. The day is memorable because I was stopped again on my way to lunch. But if that were the end of the story, we could record this scenario as a minor inconvenience that all people in the suburbs of Chicago might have to endure on occasion. Unfortunately, on my way back from lunch, I was stopped by a third officer. Before the day was over, I had been stopped by four police officers. Three were male, one was female and all were white. I never received a ticket or harsh treatment, thankfully.

Can you imagine the frustration, the anger and even the self-questioning that were unearthed inside me? Years before this incident, I had become convinced that God had called me to reconciliation and multicultural ministry. I was a minister of the gospel and more importantly a Christ follower. I cannot imagine the bitter attitudes and negative behaviors that would have come out of me had I not been tempered by the Holy Spirit living inside me at that young age of twenty-three. The Spirit's presence did not relieve me of the deflated feelings I experienced that evening after my first day of work. I reflected on the day's events and anger gave way to the comfort of the Holy Spirit. God reiterated in me that this was why my life must be committed to building bridges of reconciliation.

What I experienced that day was racism. What I envision is a world that can move from racism to gracism. Gracism, unlike racism, doesn't focus on race for negative purposes such as discrimination. Gracism focuses on race for the purpose of positive ministry and service. When the grace of God can be communicated through the beauty of race, then you have gracism. My prayer is that this book will move God's people closer to achieving such a worthy vision.

1

EVERYONE HAS A DOT

Maybe you have heard of the social experiment in which ten people were to interview at a company. Before they went to the office for the interview, a red dot was painted on one cheek of each interviewee. Each interviewee was to go into the office and sit across the desk from the interviewer. After each interview, the interviewee was debriefed. Each of the ten interviewees stated that the interviewer kept staring at the dot on his or her cheek.

Here is the kicker: Out of the ten who received a painted dot, five—unbeknownst to them—were actually given a clear dot that was not visible on their skin. Yet they still felt as if the interviewer was focusing on their dot. From this experiment we learn that people feel self-conscious about whatever makes them insecure. That insecurity might relate to one's weight, gender, race or any other distinctive that is viewed as a negative in society. Do you ever feel like people are focusing on your red dot?

When I was pulled over by police officers in the suburbs of Chicago four times within a single day, I knew that my racial dot was bright and noticeable. At first I told myself that I was being self-conscious. I tried to convince myself that race was not the issue. After the second stop, though, I knew that race was the issue whether or not I could ever prove it.

DOTISM

It's no secret that North America used to be notorious around the world for heinous acts of slavery followed by an era of institutionalized racial discrimination and segregation. Racial prejudice was a proud badge of honor for many in the United States in generations past. There was a time when only white was right and everything else from Native American, to African, to Chinese, to Jewish was wrong. But this is not the case anymore. The social acceptability of overt racism is over. By and large (notwithstanding the sovereign hand of the Almighty), it was the great struggle of blacks for their freedom, with the help of courageous whites and others, that pulled America out of the muck and mire of institutionalized bigotry.

Because our world is still racialized, racial discussions often feel forced, unsafe and either overplayed or underaddressed. When you have groups of people in a country who feel like they have dots on their face, and have been made to feel that their dots are ugly, unwanted and limiting to their success, you will also find corresponding behaviors that contribute to their self-perceptions. Many with dots feel as if they must overachieve in order to succeed in society. Some feel that hope is lost and there is no reason to strive. Hopelessness can be a weapon of mass destruction.

Over the decades many dotted people have been wrongly accused and denied employment, promotions or housing. Many people have been beaten, jailed and hung out to dry because of their dots. So after a while dotted persons understandably feel as though their dottedness is a liability. They feel as though they are being prejudged based on their facial dot.

REAL LIFE

I just returned home from consulting for a large corporate client in the heartland of the United States. One of the stories I received from an African American woman who works at the company was about her most recent racialized experience on the job. A white coworker placed a cotton plant on her desk and told her to pick it. I'm sure you can imagine how appalled the woman was. The man who did this was confronted about his distasteful act. He explained that he was simply joking.

Having spoken to the woman, it was evident to me that she didn't find the joke humorous. What was most disturbing to the black woman, as she states it, was that this man felt comfortable with this kind of joking as an acceptable prank in his work environment. After more than ten years with the company, this woman had hoped that her dot of racial distinction was vanishing.

While these kinds of racial tensions and misunderstandings still exist, minorities aren't the only ones feeling misjudged and prejudged. White males are beginning to get frustrated with what inclusion might mean for them in this increasingly multicultural society.

THE COLOR OF CHANGE

In the case of the dotted interview experiment, imagine the white male as the interviewer. After the interview one of the interviewee states, "He was staring at my dot the whole time." He is a dotist, in other words. The interviewee didn't realize that there was no dot on her face. How do you think the interviewer feels as he honestly protests that he didn't notice any dot? Both persons feel hurt and misunderstood.

WHITE MALES

America finds itself at a time in history when the white male is becoming a minority figure. The white man has a dot of his own. Some whites may already feel as if they are targeted as racists and have been silenced on issues of social justice and excluded from the table of diversity. They are beginning to feel accused and victimized by public opinion as the oppressor. There was a time when the majority of white men enjoyed their positions of power as a privilege that was unchallenged. Now the push for diversity and multiculturalism feels threatening, and many white men are wondering whether they are a part of the inclusion.

Many of my white male brothers do not want to be associated with racism, injustice or power. They are tired of being prejudged before they are even given a chance to speak. God forbid that they slip and use the wrong terminology as it relates to other races or women. These men are feeling the squeeze. Some are fully engaged in the cultural shift and welcome the opportunity to include others, while other white men are resentful and protective of positions of power and privilege. If diversity is done right, everyone—including whites—should feel welcomed at the table of ideas and leadership.

I have many white and Asian friends who have never placed a cotton plant on the desk of a black person at work, nor have they launched racial epithets at minorities. Yet they have been accused of racism simply by disagreeing with the NAACP on a stance or by questioning the policies of affirmative action in colleges or workplaces. Is this dotism or disagreement?

PLAYING THE DOT CARD

Some people's dots are invisible and yet they still see everything through the lens of their perceived dot. They feel threatened, cheated and judged, only to discover in their post-interview debriefing that dotism was not the issue at all, because the interviewer saw no dot on their face.

The interviewer wonders, "How can you accuse me of dotism? I didn't even see a dot." The interviewer also feels frustrated, threatened and judged. He doesn't see a dot on the alleged victim's face. And therein lies the struggle with race in North America. Perception versus reality; trust versus betrayal; education versus experience; relationship versus isolation. This is the context within which we find ourselves doing life and ministry, friend.

A SIN PROBLEM

Racism is not reserved for one color or culture of people. The sin of racism is an equal opportunity employer. (Or should I say an equal opportunity destroyer?) Racism is not simply a skin problem but is a sin problem. While this may sound like a cliché, we must continue to sound the alarm that God hates sin but loves sinners. Continual reminders of the spiritual impact that sin has on people, including the sin of racism, is important so that everyone can see the negative consequences that affect many. All have sinned; all can sin, regardless of race. Therefore, it is important to note that blacks can be racists too.

While walking down the street one day I heard a black man using racially pejorative language referring to Mexicans. It made me think about the universality of sin, regardless of race. Even in my own multicultural church we have to disciple people out of racist mindsets. We have heard and confronted negative racial language (much of which comes from habit) about Asians, whites, blacks and Hispanics. The most common racial giant to slay these days is prejudice against Arabs, most of whom are Muslims.

All people struggle with sins of superiority, inferiority and greed rooted in history. This includes not only Europeans, Spaniards and white Americans who perpetrated slavery but also some Africans who sold their brothers and sisters into

American slavery a hundred years ago. It further includes the many onlooking countries, corporations and religious denominations that either turned their heads or directly benefited from the horrors of American slavery.

EVERYONE HAS A DOT

We now live in a country that is pulling itself out of the muddy waters of racism as an acceptable public practice. In North America everyone has some sort of dot of distinction. Whether white, black, Mexican, female, male, gay, straight, disabled or overweight, everyone has a dot of distinction. And everyone has the capability of putting someone else down based on that person's color, culture or class. No matter its form, dotism still exists because sin still exists. And would it not be a tragedy to see people of color turn around and become the most vicious dotists of all against others? Would it not be a terrible cultural shift to see women step on the masculinity of their gender counterparts to gain their liberation? Whether the pendulum of dotism swings to one extreme or the other, it is just as debased and evil.

There must be an answer to dotism that doesn't leave people feeling left out, judged and discriminated against. There must be an answer for those in the power position who declare their innocence and swear to the world that they saw no dot on the interviewee's face. There must be a theological response to racism in the culture and racial segregation in the church. Right? There is—it's gracism.

REFLECTION QUESTIONS

1. Are you aware of your personal "red dot" (whatever makes you feel insecure around others, such as race, gender, age, weight, facial feature, emotional or physical disability)? How do you manage your feelings about it?

2. Do you sometimes try to overcompensate for your red dot when you relate to others, especially those who don't know you? If so, how?

3. Can you recall a time of discouragement or even despair over your "red dot"? What circumstances brought on those emotions?

4. Racism is a sin that can be committed by any identity group against another. How have you experienced someone making judgments about you because you were part of a certain identity group?

5. What are the factors that are helping our society to minimize dotism? What are the factors that are still promoting dotism? Which factors (one from each list) is the easiest for you to engage in?

2

From Racism to Gracism

I define racism as speaking, acting or thinking negatively about someone else solely based on that person's color, class or culture. A common definition for grace is the unmerited favor of God on humankind. Extending such favor and kindness upon other human beings is how we Christians demonstrate this grace practically from day to day. When one merges the definition of racism, which is negative, with the definition of grace, which is positive, a new term emerges—*gracism*. I define gracism as the positive extension of favor on other humans based on color, class or culture.

FAVOR OR FAVORITISM?

The extension of favor has biblical merit. The apostle Paul encouraged the Galatians, "As we have the opportunity, let us do good to all people, especially to those who belong to the family of believers" (Galatians 6:10).

The positive extension of favor toward certain people does not have to mean favoritism. When James wrote about favorit-

GRACISM

ism, he was writing in the context of loving all people and not discriminating against those who are under-resourced, low class or poor. "If you really keep the royal law found in Scripture, 'Love your neighbor as yourself,' you are doing right. But if you show favoritism, you sin and are convicted by the law as lawbreakers" (James 2:8-9).

To discriminate, exclude and not love everyone is sin. Notice that James's comments about favoritism in 2:9 follow the command to love your neighbor in 2:8. His point is that we are to love everyone and not discriminate against anyone. Does this mean that extending positive favor in an environment where everyone is loved and treated with equal respect is wrong? I say no.

Even God is shown to give extra attention to the poor, the needy, the orphans and widows throughout the whole of Scripture. Consider how God made the effort to visit Hagar in a special way even though she was a single mom who should not have been impregnated by Abram.

Hagar was a victim of Abram and Sarai's lack of faith, because they didn't believe God's promise that they would have a child. Sarai suggested that Abram sleep with Hagar as a surrogate mother to produce a child. Hagar had little say in the matter. Later, as a single mother who was impregnated by Abram, mistreated by Sarai and then cast aside as someone who was simply a baby incubator, Hagar fled into the desert to escape this intolerable situation (Genesis 16:6-7).

Notice how God proactively reached out to Hagar. "The angel of the LORD found Hagar near a spring in the desert; it was the spring that is beside the road to Shur. And he said, 'Hagar, servant of Sarai, where have you come from, and where are you going?' " (Genesis 16:7-8).

After the conversation with the angel of the Lord, Hagar "gave this name to the LORD who spoke to her: 'You are the God who sees me,' for she said, 'I have now seen the One who sees me' " (Genesis 16:13).

After this Hagar gave birth to a son named Ishmael, which means "hears." Hagar named God "the one who sees," and she had a child who she was instructed to name "hears." God hears and sees those who are marginalized and misused. Even when others don't notice you, God notices you. When others don't see you, God sees you. In those moments when it feels like no one is listening to you, God hears you and is paying attention. This is the heart of a gracist. The one who hears, sees and pays attention to those on the margins—those in the desert—is a gracist. God shows us through his actions with Hagar what the heart and art of inclusion look like.

With this new confidence, Hagar was able to return to the household from which she came because she had been graced by God. God went out of his way to minister to Hagar, an Egyptian woman who wasn't an heir to the Abrahamic promise. The Lord knew that Hagar had been a victim and was without covering, so he intentionally pursued her, listened to her, paid attention to her and communicated with her. Such understanding was all Hagar needed in order to survive in the dysfunctional home she came from. As a divine gracist, God included Hagar in his network of care by ministering to her directly from heaven.

IS GRACISM FAIR?

Is it possible to extend favor and still be fair? Distinct from favoritism, whereby one is granted favor because of a special status, ethnic superiority or commonality, gracism reaches outside the box of elitism and special favors based on some fraternal code or secret handshake. Favor is showering extra grace on a few while having love for all. Favoritism is purposefully neglecting the needs of the many to accommodate the greeds of a few. While favor is the art of inclusion, favoritism is the exercise of exclusion. Christianity is an inclusive faith that bids all to come.

Yes, it is possible to extend favor without engaging in favoritism. There is a profound difference. One is from God and the other is from human beings.

A GRACIST LESSON LEARNED

I have been teaching on gracism for a few years now. I believe that the teaching takes a while to take root. It is a slow and dawning truth that becomes clearer the more one has the opportunity to act upon it. One woman who has been listening and learning about the concept of gracism wrote me an encouraging e-mail to explain how the teaching had a surprising effect on her during an encounter she had while awaiting a flight in an airport queue.

Dear David,

Last year I was in line at the airport waiting to board my flight on Southwest Airlines. I love Southwest for their cheap fares, but the one thing I don't like is that they have no assigned seats. You can print out your boarding group pass that will have an A, B or C on it and then you wait in line till your group is called. Everyone wants a good seat on the plane, so people will stand in that line for an hour if they have to, myself included.

I was holding tightly to my boarding group pass, which said "A," and I had been waiting in that line for at least a half hour, when a family—husband, wife and two young children—loudly made their way into the "waiting to board" area. You couldn't help but notice them. They seemed confused and were talking loudly in Spanish to one another, glancing at their tickets, waving their arms and pulling their bags and their kids into the huddle of travelers. I thought perhaps they were Mexican, and I began trying to understand what they were saying, but my very limited Spanish failed me.

It's funny how these boarding group lines may not look like lines at all in the literal sense. They snake around tables, chairs and luggage; they dip with younger travelers sitting down in the middle; they have big gaps where someone has stopped to talk on his cell phone or finish a page in her novel. But just to be clear—they are indeed lines. And it is understood who is in front of you and who is in back of you, and your place in the line is respected by the other travelers. Usu-

ally. The loud Spanish speaking family was trying to work their way into the A line and ended up just a few people ahead of me, looking very confused. They were hanging just to the right of the line and you could tell they were hoping to somehow get absorbed into a real spot. The others in line were not happy about this. I watched the people get closer to one another and even position the men with them to stand on the side like a defensive line on a football team.

The Mexicans kept trying to get in, all the while looking confused, glancing at their tickets and talking in Spanish. They tried to slip in a few different places, but this line was a united front—no one was moving. All eyes were on them, and though no one said a word, the sound was deafening. I could only imagine what was going through the minds of those in line. I could see them shaking their heads in disgust. "Stupid foreigners." "Who do they think they are coming over here and just butting in?" "They have no sense." It didn't matter that no one was speaking this stuff out loud. I had heard it so many times and I could see it on their faces and in their body language. And part of me was feeling it too. I have waited in this line all this time; no way are these people gonna just butt in front of me. That's not fair! Don't they know the rules? We just don't do that here. This is my place in line.

Just as I was perfecting my speech in my head, full of righteous indignation and knowing full well that I was—we all were—right, I had a Holy Spirit smackdown. That's when a completely different thought comes into your brain that you

*know is of God and it feels like a smack upside your head. I
don't like Holy Spirit smackdowns. This time it was your voice,
David, in my head, talking about gracism. Special favor for
those who are disregarded. Special treatment, going above and
beyond to extend grace to those who have been oppressed and
dismissed in this world because of their race, class or culture.*

*It was such a powerful teaching and God used it to smack
me upside the head in that moment. I prayed silently and asked
God to help me be a gracist. He immediately showed me that
my judgment of these people was wrong. Did it really matter
who was in front of me in line? Who cares! What was most important here? What if you were in another country where you
didn't speak the language and you were confused, tired and
fearing you weren't going to make it in the plane? How would
you feel? Wouldn't you be looking for someone to show you
some kindness?*

*So I stuck my head out of line just enough to tap the Mexi-
can woman on the shoulder. "Excuse me. Please come over
here. You can get in line right here in front of me." I knew she
didn't understand my words, but my message came through
loud and clear. She smiled at me so big I thought she was going
to cry. She grabbed her husband and kids and they all kept
thanking me and bowing their heads. I saw relief come to them
as they took their spot in line in front of me. They were so
grateful and I was so ashamed. Why had it taken me so long
to do the right thing?*

David, thank you for teaching me about gracism. While I

never thought I was a racist, I see how even being silent in those moments feeds the problem. Considering others who are different and giving them special favor is unnatural for most people, but it's clearly in the Word of God, and now that I have had the chance to apply it, I can say it feels like God too.

Humbled by grace,
T. Lynn

GOD IN FRONT

When one puts a G, which stands for God, in front of the negative concept of racism, then one has begun identifying solutions and resources to address the race problem in the world. It may sound simplistic, but I believe it is right. Who said that the solution had to be difficult? Admittedly, the implementation of the solution is the most difficult. Why is this? Race problems bring with them anger, bitterness, prejudice and pride. Conversion brings with it forgiveness, patience and access to available resources, such as the filling and the fruit of the Spirit.

When we repent of our sins personally, corporately and nationally, we then can begin to rebuild on a new foundation. Radical conversion and forgiveness change the heart of a person. Therefore, unless we go through repentance over the sin of racism, we Christians are battling the problem of race just like the world, namely without God. But if Christians put God in front of any problem, that problem will diminish because God is bigger than it. I am not saying that it will keep me as a black man from getting stopped by police officers when I'm traveling in neighborhoods that make them suspicious of me, but the God in me can give me the grace to handle such incidents with patience, kindness and forgiveness.

A gracist reaches across ethnic lines and racial borders to lend assistance and "extra grace" to those who are different, on the fringe or marginalized. This person or group can be of any color, culture or gender.

Are you a gracist? The heart of a gracist extends a helping hand to those who are outside the positive norms of a particular society. While the majority may enjoy the hidden rules of a particular sociological group, gracists build bridges of inclusion for those on the margins. Just as God reached out to Hagar to comfort her in the desert of life, so we can minister to those who are desperate for someone to hear them and see them.

REFLECTION QUESTIONS

1. Can you think of an instance where you experienced favor— you were included in a positive way in what others were already experiencing? How did that giving of grace make you feel? How did you respond to those around you?

2. Can you think of a time where you were shown favoritism— others were excluded while you were included? How is your reaction to favoritism different from your reaction to favor?

3. Can you think of a time when you were excluded and others were shown favoritism? What was your reaction to that event?

4. Based on your knowledge of the Bible, do think the author's use of the term *gracism* is legitimate? Besides the example of Hagar used by the author, what other biblical stories illustrate God's gracism?

5. Can you think of a situation where you acted like a gracist— one who sees, hears or pays attention to people on the margins, extending positive ministry and service?

6. The author admits that the exercise of gracism seems too simplistic an answer for the conflicts of race and culture in our world. Yet how could the exercise of gracism at the one-on-one level help the conflicts in your world?

3

THE ART OF INCLUSION

Inclusion makes sense purely for sociological reasons based on the demographics that are facing the United States. Did you know that almost 50 percent of the American population is expected to be made up of racial and ethnic minorities by 2050? The 2000 census data confirmed that non-Hispanic whites dropped in population majority from 76 percent in 1990 to 69 percent. Three out of ten people in America are members of minority gr oups, while 6.8 million people identified themselves as multiracial on the 2000 census.

While the percentages I mention are just numbers on a page, they are represented by José, Juan, Shaquita and Lequisha in the Wal-Mart and Target stores within twenty minutes of most people's homes. Immigration has made the Hispanic population the largest minority group, surpassing blacks at 39 million, and Asians are expected to grow to 22 million by 2010 and are currently the fastest-growing minority group. This is evident by the number of Korean plazas, Chinese church signs and Japanese sushi bars popping up around the country. School populations reflect the increased minority populations to such a degree that cultural proficiency programs are becoming a must. The school system that my racially mixed kids attend not only is diverse but also is becoming more competent in furthering the dialogue needed to ensure a safe and harmonious educational experience. Black immigrants from the Caribbean and Africa now number well over one million and will triple by 2010. At the current rate, the United States will have no single majority racial or ethnic group by the middle of the twenty-first century.

I hosted a show on my radio program called *Will the Real Minority Please Stand?* The number of phone calls that came into this live program was amazing. That night, to my surprise, we had several Peruvian callers. They were calling the show to chime in on the topic with passionate and insightful thoughts on immigration. I do not know one person from Peru, but after exposure on the show, I'm interested in getting to know brothers and sisters from this group that I had no idea were so well represented in my local area. To follow up on the topic of minorities in general, I decided to host a show on Asians in particular. Again, to my surprise, Filipinos and Koreans called in. Then at one point a Mexican woman called. Since the show had to do with Asians, I asked why she had called and what point she wanted to make. She explained that she was married to a white man who was born in Asia, grew up in Africa and spoke Spanish. Wow, we are a diverse nation!

Including people from various backgrounds in our lives and ministries not only is savvy sociologically but also is biblical.

The Bible makes it clear that the Lord desires to reach people from every nation. I also believe that we need each other in order for the body to work together as God has designed his church to do and be.

A NEW VIEW

Many have come across 1 Corinthians 12 in sermons, Bible studies or casual reading of the Bible when studying the spiritual gifts or musing on biblical unity. When I was reading devotionally through the passage one time, questions related to verses 12 and 13 began to surface in my mind. I wondered why Paul, the author of this text, would include such "irrelevant" verses. I raised an eyebrow and thought that the verses didn't belong in the text at all.

In verse 12 Paul gave an analogy of the human body to illustrate his earlier point about differences regarding spiritual manifestations. He wrote, "The body is a unit, though it is made up of many parts; and though all its parts are many, they form one body. So it is with Christ" (1 Corinthians 12:12). But then, before unpacking and expanding on this analogy, Paul interjected race and culture. How forced, it seemed to me. How unpoetic. How off topic. But the truth is, the apostle purposefully put into place something important that he did not want us to miss. I had indeed missed it . . . until now. "For we were all baptized by one Spirit into one body—whether Jews or Greeks, slave or free—and we were all given the one Spirit to drink" (1 Corinthians 12:13).

Whoa! Did you notice what Paul did here? He mentioned race and culture (Jews or Greeks) and class (slave or free). He did more than simply insert an abstract thought about race and culture. The author was making a transition. He was telling us how we are to view the rest of the passage.

Paul wanted us to read verse 14 and following through the lenses of race, culture and class. To avoid reading the rest of the passage in that way would do violence to the writer's intent. Thus I appeal to you to read the next section slowly with these lenses on. Read it as if those whom you know with dots on their faces were sitting next to you. Keep race, culture and class in mind as you read.

Now the body is not made up of one part but of many. If the foot should say, "Because I am not a hand, I do not belong to the body," it would not for that reason cease to be part of the body. And if the ear should say, "Because I am not an eye, I do not belong to the body," it would not for that reason cease to be part of the body. If the whole body were an eye, where would the sense of hearing be? If the whole body were an ear, where would the sense of smell be? But in fact God has arranged the parts in the body, every one of them, just as he wanted them to be. If they were all one part, where would the body be? As it is, there are many parts, but one body.

The eye cannot say to the hand, "I don't need you!" And the head cannot say to the feet, "I don't need you!" On the contrary, those parts of the body that seem to be weaker are indispensable, and the parts that we think are less honorable we treat with special honor. And the parts that are unpresentable are treated with special modesty, while our presentable parts need no special treatment. But God has combined the members of the body and has given greater honor to the parts that lacked it, so that there should be no division in the body, but that its parts should have equal concern for each other. If one part suffers, every part suffers with it; if one part is honored, every part rejoices with it.

Now you are the body of Christ, and each one of you is a part of it. (1 Corinthians 12:14-27)

Well, what do you think? Powerful, isn't it? When we read the above text through the lenses of race, culture and class, it begins to have a clearer meaning. For me it had an entirely new meaning. I was floored when I read it afresh. I now have a new view of the passage. It has multiplied my understanding beyond the single view of addressing the diversity of spiritual gifts to affirming the multiplicity of racial, ethnic and class interdependency as well.

The writer was suggesting that we view all those in the body—those with dots, if you will—in a specific way. Anyone who may feel, look or truly be "unpresentable" or "weaker" must be handled, and even honored, differently. No one should be on the fringes without others reaching out to include them, whether white or black, Jewish or Arab, Hmong or Laotian, rich or poor, male or female.

Allow me to take creative license in paraphrasing the text using my own words and imagination. (Maybe you'd like to do the same to help you make the passage a practical reality in your friendships, fellowships and family.)

Now the body is not made up of one culture but of many. If the blacks should say to the whites, "Because I am not white, I do not belong to the body," it would not make it true. The blacks would still be a part of the body whether they vote for the same candidates or not. And if the whites should say, "Because I am not black, I do not belong to the body," it would not make it true. The whites would still be a part of the body whether they clapped their hands and shouted loudly in church or not. It doesn't mean that they are not filled with the Spirit. If the whole body was tightly structured, where would the sense of spontaneity be? If the whole body was spontaneous, where would the sense of order be? As it is, there are many parts and many cultures, but one body.

The Cuban church cannot say to the Haitian church, "I don't need you!" The Puerto Rican church cannot say to the Mexican church, "I don't need you!" The Pakistanis cannot say to the Persians, "I don't need you!" The Japanese cannot say to the Koreans, "I don't need you!" The suburban church cannot say to the urban church,

"I don't need you!" The city church cannot say to the country church, "I don't need you!" Jews cannot say to Arabs, "I don't need you!" Palestinians cannot say to Jews, "I don't need you!" On the contrary, those parts of the body that seem to be weaker are not to be dismissed or discarded as if they don't matter. They are God's special instruments of honor to reveal an aspect of God that would otherwise not be seen or experienced. There really is no part of the Christian body that is to be dismissed as unimportant. They all matter! If Palestinian Christians suffer, we all suffer. If South African Christians are freed from apartheid, we all rejoice with them. Now you are the body of Christ, and each one of you is a part of it.

PRACTICAL CHURCH GRACISM

At Bridgeway Community Church, where I pastor, we have canceled service elements, rearranged stage designs, accommodated staff positions and even added new team members with an eye to color and culture. Yes, you can call me a gracist and I won't be mad if you do! I hope I'm guilty as charged.

A gracist recognizes the beauty of diversity. A gracist will go to any length and work as diligently as possible to ensure that such beauty is seen and celebrated. A gracist truly believes that everyone matters and should be included. Gracists refuse to settle for unicultural segregation without doing all they can to include diversity at all levels of the church. This includes those in leadership and those in the pew. A gracist can't help but think about those in the neighborhood who are of a different color than are the congregants.

Imagine a local pastor asking himself or herself the following questions about the people in the target ministry area from different colors, cultures and classes. *What's wrong? Why don't they come in? What can I do to build a bridge? What is my church communicating that is keeping them away? What is my church missing by not having these people as a part of our fellowship?* These are the persistent questions of a gracist. They are good questions to ask and even tougher to answer but are important to invest brainpower and prayer power in.

Think about your church. Think about your small group or Bible class. Think about the people in your family and in your household on a daily, weekly or monthly basis. Are they all from the same color, culture or class? Now think about Christ. If he were to have a dinner party, a small Bible study group, a church service or a family meeting, do you think they would all be from the same color, culture or class? Don't we all want to be more like Christ? I am forced to ask myself, *Am I reflecting the life of Christ as a gracist or reflecting the life of a racist? Am I perpetuating segregation among Christians and simply justifying it with my preferences and comfort? Am I a bridge builder of reconciliation?* Maybe your life is lived somewhere between the two extremes. You aren't a racist and yet you've not become a gracist either. For instance, maybe you have the heart of Christ to be more inclusive but are not in a location, church or environment that allows you to regularly interact with people from a different racial, ethnic or socioeconomic background. So what are you to do?

I suggest that every person living in a unicultural environment prepare their hearts to be reconcilers in every area because the principles of God's Word, when it comes to reconciliation, work in all arenas. This includes the principle of gracism.

There are people on the fringe in your church who may be the same color as the majority of your church members but who are still in need of inclusion. There are people in your family, on your job, in your community who are in need of gracist inclusion. As you embrace and develop your calling to be a gracist, God will give you more opportunities than you can imagine to live it out. When you exercise the muscles of gracism with the marginal people you already know, your muscles will be strengthened and prepared to handle more gracist opportunities.

THE KATRINA EFFECT

A friend of mine told me about a visit to a church in Baton Rouge, Louisiana, after Hurricane Katrina hit the Gulf Coast in September 2005. The membership of the old Southern Baptist church was all white and was, as the pastor put it, plagued with some of the old mindsets of segregated thinking. The hurricane hit, and before you knew it, half a million people evacuated to Baton Rouge from New Orleans, affecting everything from the Wal-Marts to traffic patterns to church attendance. This particular white church that my friend referenced had to now live out its Christianity with approximately one hundred new black strangers attending every week. In years past the pastor had stated that the church wanted to be more multicultural; now it was a reality.

How would your church handle an influx of new people of a different race? Cultivating the soil for tomorrow so that it is ready when a multicultural seed comes to the garden of your unicultural community is a wonderful way to live. Developing a multicultural mindset before you have a multicultural ministry is important.

I know of one Christian college that wanted more people of color on their campus, so they started a scholarship athletic program. Having an athletic program can be beneficial for a college, but in this case inadequate preparation for changes in the student population wreaked havoc. The soil of the unicultural institution had not been tilled. Can you see the problems coming? Loud athletes, problems in balancing athletics with academics, interracial dating (which can often surprise an unsuspecting student body and parents), impatient professors and concerned donors all challenged the administration in unbelievable ways. Why? The unicultural soil wasn't appropriately prepared for the multicultural seed.

While a hurricane may not drive a new level of diversity to your town or church overnight, a wind of multicultural change is blowing and it behooves us all to prepare the soil so that the seed will be received well and not fall on hard ground.

DAVID THE MENACE?

I still remember how hard is was for me to shake the feelings of being a sellout when I received a nasty letter—hate mail—one day when I arrived at my office desk. The letter was riddled with words of anger, poisonous verbiage and accusation. The letter was evidently from an angry African American man who thought that my preaching, teaching and radio hosting about multiculturalism offered a dangerous and potentially harmful message for and against the black church. He called me a "menace" to the black church.

I could not disagree more. I've never read a text of Scripture that outlines God's design for a one-race church. I grew up in the black church, and I love the history and upbringing that it afforded me. My dad has been a pastor and church planter all my life. I respect the tradition of my family and the heritage it represents. Having said this, I don't believe that the Scriptures mandate a fierce protection of racial and denominational institutions. As much as I love the black church and at times miss it, there will be no black church in heaven. There will be one church and it will be multicultural. One bride, not a harem, is what Jesus is coming back for.

Do I see a role for the black church? Of course I do. Just as I see a role for ethnic churches that are catch basins for foreign-born immigrants. But this does not mean that unicultural churches that have a unique function are the end all of God's vision for his church. Such unicultural churches should still be moving toward multiculturalism in some way to prepare their members to love and reflect Christ to all people. This is the teaching of true discipleship, is it not? Did Jesus not command and commission his followers to make disciples of all nations? No church or Christian is exempt in playing a part in this magnanimous vision from on high. All churches—black, white and others—must train their members to become the gracists that God desires all his ambassadors of reconciliation to be.

Just as I am an arrow shot from my family origin into a multicultural world where I must contribute to society in an effective and godly way, so ethnic churches must see their role in preparing their members for greater multicultural influence and proficiency as Christian ambassadors. As a son of my parents and as a sibling, I can honor my parents and family history without being constrained by my family's limitations. If my parents did a good job, then I should be a well-adjusted husband, father and church leader. I can say that I have learned to be gracious and gracist because of the lessons my mother taught about forgiveness when a white neighbor kid called me a nigger continually. I learned gentleness and negotiation from my dad after he spoke privately with two of my black friends when they refused to be my friend for a summer. Dad offered each of them $1.00 and they became my friends again. How cheap I felt after I learned about this many months later! I thought I was worth at least $5.00 as a friend. Yet these same friends became even closer buddies when we were chased together through the neighborhood by white hippies who hollered obscenities at us while circling the block again and again in their hot rod with the windows down and shooting BB pellets at us. We were eight years old and were too scared to leave our hiding place in the neighborhood for hours. When Dad discovered what had happened, he called the police. Dad comforted us. I learned how to handle anger appropriately and not hysterically from my father.

I not only remember these stories from my upbringing but also I honor and celebrate the kind of family I was raised in. But just because I was raised in a unicultural family doesn't mean that I am to stay in one. In fact I am thankful to have been prepared in my unicultural family to survive and succeed in a multicultural world. It is upon that foundation that I write about gracism. My parents adequately prepared me, not poisoned me, regarding race and grace. May this be true for every unicultural environment, families and churches in particular.

How does one prepare the soil? How do churches raise a generation of gracists? What can each of us do to be a gracist? The next several chapters address specific behaviors that can help one live out the principles of gracism in a practical way.

I have identified seven phrases from 1 Corinthians 12 as gracist sayings. Chapters four through ten will address each saying in turn and give us clear suggestions on how to integrate the sayings into daily action. I have emphasized in italicized type the sayings in the text below.

Those parts of the body that seem to be weaker are indispensable, and the parts that we think are less honorable we treat with *special honor*. And the parts that are unpresentable are treated with *special modesty*, while our presentable parts need *no special treatment*. But God has combined the members of the body and has given *greater honor* to the parts that lacked it, so that there should be *no division in the body*, but that its parts should have *equal concern* for each other. If one part suffers, every part suffers with it; if one part is honored, every part *rejoices with it*. (1 Corinthians 12:22-26, emphasis added)

SEVEN SAYINGS OF A GRACIST

1. "SPECIAL HONOR"—lifting up the humble among us. *I will lift you up.*

2. "SPECIAL MODESTY"—protecting the most vulnerable among us from embarrassment. *I will cover you.*

3. "NO SPECIAL TREATMENT"—refusing to accept special treatment if it is at the detriment of others who need it. *I will share with you.*

4. "GREATER HONOR"—God, as a gracist, has given greater honor to the humble. *I will honor you.*

5. "NO DIVISION"—when the majority helps the minority, and the stronger help the weaker (gracism), it keeps us from division within the body (an opposite view than normal). *I will stand with you.*

6. "EQUAL CONCERN"—having a heart as big for our neighbors as we do for ourselves. *I will consider you.*

7. "REJOICES WITH IT"—when the humble, or less honorable, are helped, we are to rejoice with them. (It's easier to weep with those who weep than to rejoice with those who rejoice.) *I will celebrate with you.*

REFLECTION QUESTIONS

1. How have you seen the increase in minority populations where you live? List from three to five places or instances where you have noticed it.

2. If you have a Wal-Mart or Target in your area, take an hour and sit in the snack or coffee bar and mark on a sheet of paper the different groups of people you are able to identify. What surprised you in this experiment? Besides English, how many other languages did you hear? How has this exercise supported or contradicted the author's contention of increased cultural diversity?

3. Read 1 Corinthians 12 slowly. How does the inclusion of culture and class change how you apply this passage?

4. The author stated, "A gracist can't help but think about those in the neighborhood who are of a different color than are the congregants." After your Wal-Mart or Target experiment, compare your observations of the store's level of diversity of

customers to the level of diversity of your church's congregation. Which is more diverse? Which institution, based on 1 Corinthians 12, should be more diverse? Why does this difference not bother most churches and their leaders? Should it bother them? Why or why not?

4

SAYING ONE: "I WILL LIFT YOU UP"

(Special Honor)

Those parts of the body that seem to be weaker are indispensable,
and the parts that we think are less honorable we treat with special honor.

1 CORINTHIANS 12:22-23 (EMPHASIS ADDED)

In 1 Corinthians 12:23 we see the apostle Paul refer to treating others with "special honor." This means saying to others, "I will lift you up." A gracist is committed to lifting up others who are on the fringes, in the minority or in need of extra attention.

Paul was saying that the people who have less honor because, let's say, their gifts lack public pizzazz, or their pedigree is less than glowing, are the ones who need special honor. Sometimes we have to work hard to discover and lift up those seemingly hard-to-notice people who don't shine like the stars around us.

In my pastoral ministry many of the people I work alongside

are extremely gifted and skilled. They are the easier people to recognize. It takes extra work for me to scope out the hidden heroes. These are those servants who are making a major difference for the kingdom of God and yet are often overlooked. Such people may include volunteers in our children's ministry, folks working in the parking lots, servants on our technical team or someone at an office work station who keeps the administrative details of business in order.

Such individuals may seem weaker or not as important because they are not as visible. While none of us would openly call them weaker or dispensable, the way we act toward them or neglect them is evidence of their near invisibility.

SAFE HAVEN

BridgeKids is our children's ministry at Bridgeway Community Church. Within BridgeKids a new ministry called Safe Haven has been gaining steam. Safe Haven serves children who are disabled, are mentally challenged or fall somewhere on the autism spectrum. Because children who have special needs are also in need of special attention, we provide this service as a ministry to parents who desire to worship in the main auditorium with other adults. Safe Haven is not only a blessing to the parents, but moreover it is a blessing to the special needs children. Our desire as a church is to minister to children with special needs in such a way that they can experience the love of Christ in whatever manner they are able to receive it.

It wasn't until I held a fireside leadership chat with the ministry team of BridgeKids that I realized I had been missing the opportunity to lift up a special group in our midst. The woman who leads the ministry has an autistic son, and she explained her vision with passion and emotion while painting for me a picture of what could be. "Pastor," she pleaded, "these children are a full part of the body here at Bridgeway and we need to help them understand their value to the entire church family and the unique contribution they can make to our church." I was floored by our prior neglect and inspired by the vision to lift up a "weaker" group among us. It was a big "Aha!" for me.

In that very meeting I began drilling down into the idea of special needs ministry for children and their families with a myriad of questions about an autistic child's ability to understand, interact, minister and feel the love of Christ. I affirmed our children's ministry in my office that day and was encouraged by the hearts of our servants. Moreover, I was excited about maximizing the ideas and impact that we can have on and through children who have special needs. Such a focus will need support, education and awareness, along with dedicated space and resources, to raise Safe Haven to full capacity. Lifting them and their needs up to the surface of our overall ministry is something I am fired up about.

The Scripture writer reminded us that no one is dispensable. In fact everyone who is a part of the body is necessary. There are no people groups on the planet who do not matter. Everyone should be included in the circle of honor, regardless of color, class, culture, popularity, giftedness or personality. This was exactly Paul's point. We are to lift others up. Remember to include everyone in your circle of honor because God in Christ included you.

BART AND BIG BILL

After thirty-three years as a state trooper for the state of Maryland, Officer Richard Wilson (also known as Bart) accepted the invitation of his girlfriend to attend Bridgeway Community Church, the church I pastor in Columbia, Maryland. Bart didn't know the Lord, nor did he want to visit Bridgeway. His girlfriend, however, made a deal with him. "If you visit Bridgeway and find one thing wrong that you don't like," she said, "then you never have to attend again and I'll stop hounding you." Bart saw this as a great deal. He reveled in the fact that he had to identify only one thing that displeased him and he could resume his regular Sunday habits of working on his car and watching football. Little did Bart know what God had in store.

I don't remember the sermon I preached on that Sunday, but I do remember extending an invitation for anyone in the congregation who wanted to receive Jesus Christ, as I periodically do as the Lord leads. God had a plan for Bart on this particular Sunday. As I extended the gospel invitation for salvation, Bart felt his legs stand him straight up. "As if I were the only sinner in the room," Bart states, "I felt God calling me to repentance specifically and personally." What a beautiful day that was for Bart, for his girlfriend and for me as I led the congregation in a prayer to place faith in Jesus Christ! This was the day Bart crossed over from spiritual death to spiritual life.

As a new Christian, Bart was excited and ready to do life God's way. Turning away from the behaviors of his state trooper days and the sins of his youth, Bart turned to the church to serve. He alerted the church office that he didn't have skills to sing, dance, act or preach, but if the church needed someone to move chairs, run errands, carry things or transport people, he would be more than happy to serve in this way. One day my executive assistant asked Bart to drive me to the airport so that a staff member would not have to do so. Shortly thereafter Bart offered to drive me anywhere. He explained that he had driven for many official people, including the governor of our state. Bart convinced me that serving through driving was in no way imposing on him but, conversely, he would be more than happy to transport me to my weekly radio show fifty miles from my house, to airports, meetings and events throughout the major cities near our church, such as Washington, D.C., Baltimore, Philadelphia and New York. What a godsend! Who knew?

Subsequently Bart began driving me in his personal vehicle to ministry events. Or he did until another member of the congregation, a man known as Big Bill who owns a limo company, offered me his vehicles as his own personal ministry. Can you believe that? This offer was totally unexpected and unrelated to the driver whom God had provided for me just weeks prior. Big Bill required, however, that I use his employed drivers due to insurance requirements and asked that his gift of service be anonymous. I committed to being discreet about his generosity, but I couldn't commit to using only his drivers, since God had already provided me with one who had decades of experience driving all kinds of people. After sharing this with the limo company owner, he agreed to allow his cars to be available for Bart's use in transporting me since he was a retired state trooper. I was amazed by God's grace. At first I struggled with whether or not I, as a minister, should even embrace this gift of service. After careful consideration, why would I deny what God has clearly offered me as a blessing? I have fully embraced this gift with thanksgiving while trying to be as modest as I can.

Blessed with a car and a driver through no finagling of my own, I unwittingly discovered how much I am taking advantage of this ministry as a stewardship opportunity in my life. While en route I prepare for appointments, review material for the radio show and conduct meetings with people. Sometimes, when I am alone except for Bart, I just pray, reflect or daydream while looking out the window. What a crazy and unlikely gift— one that I didn't even realize could be leveraged for ministry and would never have solicited for myself! That's just like God, isn't it? God lifted me up in a very unique and specific way.

You may not have a car and driver, but you do need someone to lift you up in specific ways that meet your particular needs, right? God is the master planner and knows just how to configure his people in such a way as to meet your every need. Do you believe this?

PRAYER

One practical way we can lift each other up is through prayer. Interceding on behalf of others who are underappreciated, undervalued, on the fringes or different is a great way to elevate your care and concern for them. In relating gracefully to someone you are reaching out to, simply ask this person regularly about how you can pray for him or her. The next time you speak with the person you are lifting up, ask how things are going regarding the prayers that were requested. This person will be blessed to know that someone is lifting him or her up in prayer. We all are blessed by the intercession of others, but for those on the margins it feels even more rewarding to know that someone in the majority culture or a power position cares enough to be concerned with such matters.

In addition, to take the prayers of gracism to a higher level, ask the person to whom you are reaching out to pray for you. This takes you out of the superior position and places you under the grace and spiritual support of someone else who may otherwise have perceived that you are not in need of him or her but are there only to reach out. The exchange of gifts and the mutuality of lifts give dignity to human relationships. When I lift you up, you are blessed. Likewise, when I allow you to lift me up, while it may be humbling for me, it is dignifying for you.

Remember when Jesus asked the woman at the well for a drink of water (John 4:7)? Jesus started the exchange by asking for something he needed. How dignifying! This woman who may have lost all self-respect and dignity must have been amazed by the fact that she was being asked to meet a Jewish man's need at the community well. Everyone has something to offer. Unfortunately, when we are in the power position, it becomes increasingly difficult to allow ourselves to be served in a spiritual way. Yet Jesus allowed himself to be served by this Samaritan woman.

The apostle Peter had a hard time with this lesson when it was time for another water lesson. This time it had to do with Jesus washing his feet (John 13:1-10). Peter thought it humiliating to allow himself to be served by Jesus. Yet Jesus clearly communicated to Peter that this must be done, not because Jesus needed dignifying like the woman at the well, but because Peter needed humbling.

Lifting up, in part, includes elevating others and humbling ourselves by allowing others to elevate us. Imagine a group of people lifting one another up and allowing themselves to be lifted up. In a community of lifters no one would feel compelled to exalt themselves. Instead it would be an environment of special honor.

ELEVATORS OF GRACE

I was at Heathrow Airport, in London, at the time of this writing. When it was time for me to go from the train to the plane, I needed to elevate from one floor to another. In the United States we call lifting devices affixed in shafts in the wall *elevators*. The purpose of the elevator is to lift up a person or group of people from one floor to the next. In London, however, elevators have a different name. They are called *lifts*. Having stepped onto a lift, I ascended from the train level to the plane level. *How fitting an analogy!* I thought. This is exactly what my role in the lives of people, especially those on the fringes, should be. Would it not be a wonderful thing for believers to picture themselves as uplifters to help others move toward their plane in life so they can fly above their circumstances?

Practically speaking, lifting others can be done by raising a voice for those who do not have a voice. When the children's ministry leader spoke up for the autistic and disabled community, she was raising a voice for those who were not sitting at the table of decision. Who is speaking for the Latinos, African Americans, Asians, females or children at the board room tables in your church? Is there is a family of a different culture in your majority-race neighborhood who you can reach out to and invite over for dinner? A gracist would say, "Send me, Lord."

CAUTION

When attempting to be a lifter in the lives of others, please make sure that you serve others in a manner that is received by them as honoring and is not perceived as honoring only from your perspective. I can't help but think of all the times I tried to honor my wife with gifts that I thought were just perfect, only to realize that the gifts were more to my liking than hers. Yikes!

One time I bought Amber what I thought was the best gift ever. It was her birthday and I thought she would love the rice cooker I purchased. As a guy I had no idea that kitchen appliances didn't fall into the category of personal gifts. (Yes, ladies, you can laugh now.) What's worse is that one year I purchased some special lingerie for my wife. I thought I was "the man." Well, you guessed it, I was acting like the man—or a typical male, I should say. I fell to the illusion that this was a great personal gift for my wife. Amber (who gave me permission to share this story with you) educated me by informing me that such gifts were really for my benefit. She actually loves to receive these kinds of gifts but would prefer them to be given when it is not her birthday. If I do desire to purchase a cooking appliance or lingerie for her birthday, I am to make sure that it is coupled with another, more personal gift that is truly for her benefit. I have learned that such gifts include a manicure, a pedicure, a spa treatment while I keep the kids, shopping gift cards and many other things that I've stored in my mental computer.

In Amber's mind, while my motives were right in giving her birthday gifts (okay, partially right), my method of gift giving was more self-centered than spouse-centered. Likewise, when we serve others, we must be careful to ensure that we are doing what is truly best for them and not best for us. Because our motives are often convoluted, we can psych ourselves into believing that we are lifting others up and doing good for them when the reality is that we are looking for our own pats on the back about our advocacy, our gratification and our desires.

I have learned that the best way to avoid such embarrassing

moments is to simply ask people the best way to serve, inspire, help or lift them.

ADOPTION VERSUS PARTNERING

My church was on a mission to reach a community in Kenya, Africa, and adopt a local community within our county where we could serve. We desired to identify one community where we could clean up, feed the hungry, advocate for people politically and carry out programs for the young people. Immediately after I cast a vision for reaching out to the local community we had identified, a leader pulled me aside and said, "David, we should avoid the term *adopt* and use the term *partner*." I inquired as to why, and he explained that adoption sounds like we just want to descend on the community as their messiah to serve them without any of their input or will. That leader was exactly right. I hadn't thought about how we were perceived or how the community in my county or in Kenya would receive our good works. Again, I was being self-centered in my attempt to lift others up without even realizing it.

After being confronted about this, I immediately changed our language and approach. I empowered our volunteers to go into the community and to the county executive's office to ask them how we could serve. We consulted the community by going from door to door and asking people what their needs were and giving them the ownership to leverage our volunteers and money to help minister to their own community. In addition we met with the leaders in Kenya and came alongside them to partner on reaching their villages in the best manner that they themselves prescribed. Their leaders knew exactly what was needed much better than we did. Now in Kenya the leaders of over forty churches have committed to multitribal ministry and have erected a school and orphanage that we have been integral in partnering with toward success. Praise God!

SPECIAL HONORS AWARD

Bart and Big Bill, the men who make it possible for me to have a car and driver, are both behind-the-scenes servants who meet a unique and specific need. These are not the kinds of people who normally receive public praise unless they are called out and given special honor. In many ways these gentlemen have been lifters in my life. They are elevators of grace. Likewise I try my best to lift them up in ways that elevate them to higher levels of blessing in their lives.

Paul alerted us to the fact that such servants, people who may seem weaker or lesser in any way, are perfect candidates for a special honor award. These two brothers definitely qualify for the nomination of this award. And by the way, driving the pastor around is not a glorious job when you as the driver must sit in the car and wait or, worse, circle on the busy streets of New York or Washington for hours until the pastor comes out of a session. This is the kind of service that the public doesn't see but God does.

The servants in our Safe Haven ministry qualify as candidates for the special honor award too. They may not be seen with food splattered on their clothing, enduring unpredictable behaviors from mentally challenged children, but God sees them. Such an award should be given by a committee of gracists who are seeking out hidden heroes who would never nominate themselves. My prayer is that God will lift your eyes to notice silent servants in your families, churches and communities. By honoring them you will be honoring God.

Is it not always a beautiful thing to lift up those who are weaker, lesser known, on the outskirts of public praise, in the background of social mores or living behind the curtains of onstage applause? Is it not the responsibility of the majority to lift up the minority? Is it not the responsibility of the stronger to lift up the weaker? Is it not required of those in power to help those who are outside of power? Would God not desire for the in crowd to reach out to those who are crowded out?

LEAD US NOT INTO TEMPTATION

In addition, by lifting up those who are in the background and on the fringes, whether they are racial minorities, silent servants, a woman in a crowd of men, a single person among a coupled gathering or a Sunday morning visitor, we bless them in a way that doesn't tempt or compel them to feel like they must lift themselves up. Because Jesus teaches us not to exalt ourselves, it is of great importance that we exalt Christ and honor one another.

The Bible says,

Let another praise you, and not your own mouth;
someone else, and not your own lips. (Proverbs 27:2)

I wonder if those who often struggle with interjecting themselves into conversations at parties, and those who feel the need to be self-promotional, are doing so because we fail to recognize their contributions. What would happen if we were to release a force of encouragers—gracists, if you will—and people who were radically inclusive? Can you imagine what would happen if those on the sidelines of popularity and preferences were actually valued, included and inspired to join the ranks of the celebrated? What would happen to their spirits of discouragement, depression and disillusionment?

My guess is that walls of separation between our churches would shatter. I believe that people would not have to fight for themselves if we would stand up for one another. Racially speaking, I would love to see white, black, Asian and Latino churches become elevators of grace to one another. It would do my heart good to see churches wash the feet of one another across denominational and racial lines. Would it not bless the heart of God to see his multicultural family of believers commit to lifting up each other on purpose, with purpose, for a divine purpose? In so doing we will not only bless God and each other, but also we will not lead each other into the temptation of competition, self-advocacy and a kind of self-promotion that reeks of denominational or ethnic pride.

WHEN THE WALLS COME DOWN

Once the walls come down, we still have to live together. This is where the rubber meets the road. How are we to live together when the melting pot of black, white, Latino, Arab, Asian, young, old, rich, poor, Democrat, Republican, blue and white collar all converge—or crash—in the same church? It is sometimes true that when the walls come down the gloves come off. Sometimes exposure to different cultures, styles and preferences may clash with one's personal likes and dislikes. What happens when the elevator gets crowded? Multicultural ministry takes real work, as we will discover in the next several chapters.

REFLECTION QUESTIONS

1. Within the walls of your church as it is now, who are the marginalized people—who are not "in"? The poor? The less educated? The teenagers? The singles? Those divorced? Single mothers? Identify at least two marginalized groups within your church. How can you be an ambassador of reconciliation to that group? How can you educate yourself about them?

2. The author states, "I have learned that the best way to avoid such embarrassing moments is to simply ask the best way to serve, inspire, help or lift them." What is one gift of kindness you could do for your prayer partner that would truly meet his or her need without causing humiliation?

3. Who are the people in your church who deserve special honor awards? Are there other people in your life—parents, spouses, neighbors, teachers—who deserve special honor awards? Buy a box of thank-you cards and one evening sit down to write special honor award notes.

4. Are there any people whom you feel should be excluded from the circle of honor? Why?

5. Who are the people you usually are drawn to lift up? What is it about them that draws you? Are there other important characteristics that you might be excluding but that you should recognize?

5

SAYING TWO: "I WILL COVER YOU"

(Special Modesty)

The parts that are unpresentable are treated with special modesty,
while our presentable parts need no special treatment.

1 CORINTHIANS 12:23-24 (EMPHASIS ADDED)

Modesty is not a term that our generation is accustomed to using in its everyday vocabulary. When was the last time you heard it used outside a sermon encouraging women to watch how they dress? In the Bible the term was primarily used by the apostle Paul to address how a woman should wear her hair or clothing in public settings so as not to draw attention to her vulnerabilities, private areas of beauty or exposures that were appropriate only for her husband. Apostles Paul and Peter even suggested that there was a way a woman could wear her hair that could cause men to look on her longingly and a way she could comb it that would be more modest in its presentation so as to not draw the attention of the opposite sex (1 Corinthians 11:13-15; 1 Peter 3:3-4).

While the culture of the day dictates the specific limits between modesty and immodesty, the overall principle of modesty, or covering one's vulnerabilities, is one that transcends time and culture. Some things are appropriate for the public eye and some things need to stay behind closed doors.

STAY-AT-HOME DRESS

One day my wife asked me about a new dress she was trying on to see how well it fit and whether she should wear it to an event we were to attend. She wanted my honest opinion about the dress, which is seldom a win-win situation for a guy. I responded to my wife's inquiry about how the dress looked by saying, "That dress looks so good that I believe it's a stay-at-home dress." What was I saying to my wife? I was telling her that I liked the dress personally, but it wasn't appropriate for others to see. There are times when I have sought Amber's opinion about my clothes and she has been honest enough to tell me that certain clothes don't compliment me. Certain clothing fits my body type more than others. A part of the beauty of clothing is that it can cover the areas we are least proud of. The truth is that we all have vulnerabilities, blemishes, embarrassing spots and weaker assets as well as beauty areas that should be kept private.

Likewise the body of Christ needs to learn how to cover itself with the clothing of grace. In fact Paul wrote to the Colossians that they were to clothe themselves with "compassion, kindness, humility, gentleness and patience" (Colossians 3:12). The behaviors and attitudes that Paul mentioned in Colossians are the attributes that body members ought to have toward each other across racial, ethnic and class lines. At first you may think I'm stretching the meaning of the verse, but notice with me the verse that leads to the above statement about clothing the body: "Here there is no Greek or Jew, circumcised or uncircumcised, barbarian, Scythian, slave or free, but Christ is all, and is in all" (Colossians 3:11). Did you notice that Paul mentioned race, religious practice, ethnicity and class in verse 11? Then to top off the message he began verse 12 with the word "Therefore," meaning "Based on what I have just stated in the previous verses." So the verse reads like this: "Therefore, as God's chosen people, holy and dearly loved, clothe yourselves with compassion, kindness, humility, gentleness and patience."

The call to cover one another is the call to express godly attitudes before judging or exposing areas of the body that are blemished or unseemly. When you and I are hurt by another part of the body, we are to handle it in a way that is clothed with the aforementioned attitudes and behaviors. There are some "stay at home" issues in the body of Christ and even among our cultural, racial and denominational groups that need to be dealt with behind closed doors in a healthy manner. I don't say this to imply that the church should sweep sin under the rug or refuse to address matters of immorality or abuse. That can only lead to more sin and abuse. My point is that we must not air the dirty laundry immediately, especially as it relates to race. Modesty in the way we speak about ethnic groups, genders and classes is critical to unity. While we may want to blast a particular group within the body of Christ because we disagree with their theology, methodology, politics or philosophy of ministry, it may behoove us to reconsider how we speak about them. We must ensure that we have the clothing of grace on to cover parts of our body that are vulnerable and blemished.

TAKING AIM

I remember one author whose material I read in Bible college and who seemed to want to take aim at every part of the body of Christ that didn't agree with his own biblical view. When he criticized the various parts of the body without the clothing of grace on, it became hurtful and divisive. A pastor friend of mine was a victim of this author's attack. While the author's book took aim at the style of ministry my pastor friend was leading, I don't believe the author realized that he was being careless and divisive. When my pastor friend was asked in a staff meeting whether he was going to write a book or article to retort, he responded by saying, "There is nothing the devil would like to see more than two high-profile Christian leaders publicly fighting. I will not be used that way, and the non-Christian world would be distracted by that kind of testimony." I was impressed by this mature response. I can also tell you that my pastor friend and another Christian leader sat down with the author to address the matters behind closed doors in search of reconciliation.

The principle is this: when you or I have the power to criticize another denomination, ministry, class or group, let's not take aim and fire. Let's power down and cover the body of Christ with compassion, kindness, humility, gentleness and patience. Attitudes and behaviors such as these will lead us down the road to reconciliation much faster.

Paul continued in Colossians 3:13-14 to encourage forbearance and forgiveness, followed up by love to cover all the virtues so that perfect unity will be the result. Perfect unity involves the areas of difference listed in verse 11, which include but are not limited to race, ethnicity, religious rituals and class.

SPECIAL MODESTY

Paul's words about clothing in the book of Colossians shed light on the importance of his message about modesty in 1 Corinthians. The apostle said that those who are "unpresentable" should be covered with special modesty. This means that there are times when those who aren't the popular race or church or the powerful class may need to be covered, shielded or advocated for. There are times when it would be easy for those who are more powerful and popular to use their capabilities to embarrass the dignity of those who would otherwise be easily exposed. This is what the unwise author I spoke about earlier did to my pastor friend as well as many other victims in his sights, including groups like charismatic Christians, Christian counselors and the contemporary worship movement within churches across North America. I believe it is incumbent upon those with power or privilege to take on the responsibility to protect and cover those who don't have them.

When my wife questioned me about her dress, it was important for me to protect my wife's dignity, not because I'm more powerful or popular, but because I could see her from a privileged position and have insights that can speak into her life as others cannot. Had I responded by saying, "I don't care what you wear; you're not my wife," that would have crushed her.

I wonder if we say that to each other in the body of Christ. May we never be comfortable saying, "I don't care what the Methodist church down the street does; they are not my denomination" or "I don't care what the white church five miles away does; they are not my spiritual siblings." I believe that such statements would horrify Christ as much as my wife would be horrified had I said I didn't care about her dress and divorced myself emotionally from her concerns and well-being. Do we do this regarding race and class? Do we say about those who are poor, "Oh well, they made their bed; now they must sleep in it." May it never be!

You see, friends, if we don't care about each other, then we will not cover each other. While I may have a different level of concern about what your spouse wears, I'm intimately concerned with what my spouse wears because I am emotionally invested in and spiritually connected to her. Should it not be the same within the body of Christ? If so, then let's cover one another with modesty.

Had I given my wife the green light to wear that dress, I

would have let her go out of the house unshielded, exposed
and immodest, which would not have been responsible for me
as her husband. I understand that the dress analogy is a minor
example to make a major point, but how about something
more substantive and severe like a teenage child who is having
a personal struggle? To what degree do I as a parent share the
details of my child's personal business with other church members? One's child needs to be covered too, right? He or she
needs the dignity of privacy and special modesty. There are
ways for a parent to share struggles generally without embarrassing his or her child in the public gaze.

Paul said that there are those among us who need special
modesty. Gracism demands that we take those who are marginalized as minorities and ensure that they are covered and protected from embarrassment where possible.

Can you imagine a visitor attending a church and tripping
down the aisle on the way in? That would be embarrassing.
Now imagine that later in the service someone from the stage,
such as the worship leader or pastor, refers to the tripping spell
in a joking way. That would be cold, heartless and embarrassing
humor at the expense of the guest. Not cool, right? Now consider that the person is not only a visitor but is one of a mere
five Asian people in a gathering of a couple hundred people.
Courtesy would require that we refrain from leveling humor at
someone else's expense anyway. Hospitality, however, would require that we bend over backward to help a guest. Gracism demands even more. Gracism requires that I increase my sensitiv-

ity level to the guest because of his minority status, understanding that he is also unofficially representing other Asians by virtue of association, whether spoken or unspoken, welcome or unwelcome, fair or unfair. It is the reality of being in the minority position and is the weight carried by many. Just as Christians carry the weight of their testimony as Christ followers and represent, whether officially or unofficially, their Lord and the reputation of others who call themselves Christians, so minorities carry with them the weight of those they represent.

THE EMBARRASSMENT FACTOR

In light of this, what is special modesty? It is the special sensitivity toward minorities in whatever form they may come to this status—white, black, visitors, foreigners, religious, marginalized, disabled, nonassertive and so on—to ensure that their reputations and dignity are taken into account before (if ever) exposing their weaknesses, blemishes or vulnerabilities.

The point I am emphasizing is that those who are in the minority position have a higher embarrassment factor due to their status. For instance, if a white male finds himself in a gathering that is populated by a majority of African American females, he is vulnerable to a greater level of embarrassment than if he were in a homogeneous white environment. Therefore, it is the responsibility of the gracist to ensure that he is protected, covered and cared for with extra grace that may not be required for others in the room. Gracists take on the job of caring for the marginalized regardless of their color, class or culture. They intentionally reach out to those who are on the fringe, and if for some reason the marginalized person or group falters, gracism demands covering that person in such a way that his dignity is protected and his faults are not exploited.

How different would your life be if you lived each day committed to the dignity of those around you, especially those in need of extra care? What would such a day look like in your world? Instead of families, communities and churches being filled with backbiting or suspicion, how about their being places where believers seek to help each other look and feel their best? How about an environment where I seek to help you succeed and you seek to encourage me? Or more, if I fall or fail, will you exploit and embarrass me because you can, or will you cover me? Is there not a balance somewhere between my sanctification and my missteps? If I ask the wrong question, use the wrong racial language or hold an unpopular social view, will you call me a racist or sexist, or will you cover me while inspiring me to new levels of education and growth? These questions are poignant because they get to the heart of what it means to cover others who haven't been fully enlightened or sanctified.

Like a child who needs protection, so many people in the maturation process of race relations also need room to struggle, grow, disagree and fail. The principle of covering people or giving them this space to mature in matters of reconciliation is extremely important to the safety of their process, lest their multicultural growth be stunted.

Paul exhorted the believers in Corinth to offer special modesty to those on the outer rings of social and cultural acceptability. In order to live out the kind of lifestyle that suppresses our human desire to gossip, slander, put down and expose the weaknesses and faults of others, Paul was lobbying for a new kind of faith expression. One where care and concern for the reputation of the minority, or the weaker one, is taken into account.

REFLECTION QUESTIONS

1. How much value does our society place on the virtue of modesty? How does this impact our ability to be sensitive to care for the modesty of others?

2. What biblical examples can you think of where one person in the power position did not embarrass or shame someone in a weaker position but rather protected, cared for or shielded that person?

3. How could exposing people hurt their spiritual growth? How could it help them? What are the standards you use to know which action to take?

4. Journal about an event in your past when someone else stood up for your reputation or protected you from others' judgment. What emotions did you feel?

6

SAYING THREE: "I WILL SHARE WITH YOU"
(No Special Treatment)

The parts that are unpresentable are treated with special modesty,
while our presentable parts need no special treatment.

1 CORINTHIANS 12:23-24 (EMPHASIS ADDED)

I was flying home from England with a good friend, Rick, whom I had been traveling with across the world to build bridges of reconciliation. We were on a major airline. All had gone smoothly in our travels from Africa to Europe, but in London it became apparent that there was a mix-up with our tickets. I was ticketed for economy, which was the way it was supposed to be, but Rick's ticket was clearly for business class on this final leg from London to Baltimore. Because of administrative errors, Rick's itinerary in the airline computer stated that he was to be seated in the economy class with me. After speaking to the counter worker, Rick was told that he could take a later flight on which the airline would correct the error so that he could sit in the comfort of business class. The only other option was for Rick to sit in economy class, where he would be squeezed in with the rest of us.

COMFORT OR COMMUNITY?

What would you do? Put yourself in Rick's shoes where you have the privilege to upgrade and take another flight that would get you home in about the same amount of time. You have the status, the history, the airline points accumulated and the right to ride in a more comfortable class. The only downside is that you would not be able to fly with your associate. You would lose the opportunity to share in fellowship with your friend. You would get to experience the comforts of the nicer class but would do so alone. What choice would you make in this scenario? What did Rick do?

To my surprise, Rick chose to ride with me in economy for the seven-hour journey. He wasn't happy about the mistake the airline had made, but he was pleased to ride with me. The choice seemed easy for him once he got over his frustration at the airline's error coming at the end of a long trip. Once Rick gathered his thoughts and made a value judgment between comfort and community, he chose community. Rick would rather fly with his friend than fly alone. The comforts of flying solo didn't override his desire for community and companionship.

The apostle Paul said, "The parts that are unpresentable are treated with special modesty, while our presentable parts need

no special treatment" (1 Corinthians 12:23-24, emphasis added).
While special modesty says, "I will cover you," the phrase "no special treatment" says, "I refuse to accept favors or perks that may hurt you," even if the refusal is emotionally difficult. If my choice to express my rights, freedoms and privileges will chip away at your dignity, then I will think twice about exercising that right in that moment. This does not mean that I cannot enjoy the privileges and luxuries of life, but it does take into account how and when I enjoy those privileges and luxuries. If my acceptance of special favors makes you feel less dignified or put down, then I'll pass on the favor and share in your experience.

The third saying of Paul in 1 Corinthians 12 may be the hardest principle of gracism to accept because it cuts to the heart of our insatiable appetites for entitlement and the expression of individual freedom. The concept of downshifting, downgrading or refusing to accept special treatment is antithetical to Western individualism and assaults much of what we have been taught as being our inalienable rights. Downgrading in order to share in community is countercultural to upward mobility and personal aggrandizement.

While I am in no way arguing for communism, I am saying that when you and I have a choice to either share in community or enjoy special treatment that would leave others out, we are put into a quandary. Such intersections can be dealt with in only one of two ways. Either "I will lift you up," as the first saying goes, or "I will share with you" in community, as the third saying proclaims.

Often sharing is defined as giving a part of what I have to someone else who doesn't have it. If you are hungry and I have a slice of bread, then sharing would be me giving a piece of my bread to you so that you too can eat.

I sense that the nuance of sharing Paul was speaking about in this passage is the sharing of common experiences. It is not simply giving to those in the body who do not have. Rather, it is majority persons refusing to accept special treatment, perks and honors that are unnecessary in the face of those who do not have them. Accepting such "in-your-face" special treatment is the opposite of humility and grace. Though it may feel good to be special and above the rest, power and prestige can be addictive drugs that rob others of life's basics.

GETTING A PIECE OF THE PIE

Imagine a line of church members waiting to get a plate of food at a church dinner. Let's say there are fifty members and five guests. Because the members know where the food is, know the process of getting the food and know the house rules, they have the advantage of eating first. They also know that there are typically not enough desserts at these monthly functions. Most of the insiders are aware of this and have come up with a system to ensure that they get their piece of the pie. While getting their meal in line, they have the cook in the back set aside some pie for them in the kitchen. When it's time for dessert, the five guests who are unaware of the inside information lose out on getting any pie.

What happened here? The insiders—majority persons—had the knowledge and networks to make the system of ascertaining dessert work in their favor. There was no crime committed, no one hurt physically or financially, no massive act of discrimination levied against the visitors. The uninformed guests simply didn't get to enjoy a piece of the pie because the majority players had inside knowledge and received special treatment.

1 Corinthians 11

While the illustration I gave above is a modern-day example of how people on the fringes of community can be left out, Paul built the concepts of gracism on real-life examples that came out of the divided church in Corinth. In chapter 11 Paul rebuked the Corinthians for discriminating against those who had no inside knowledge or favor. He brought correction on the majority for enjoying food with special treatment while others were last in line and some didn't get to eat at the church dinner at all. The greedy appetites of the in crowd failed to include those in the out crowd.

Here is Paul's criticism toward the Corinthians in his own words. "When you come together, it is not the Lord's Supper you eat, for as you eat, each of you goes ahead without waiting for anybody else. One remains hungry, another gets drunk. Don't you have homes to eat and drink in? Or do you despise the church of God and humiliate those who have nothing? What shall I say to you? Shall I praise you for this? Certainly not!" (1 Corinthians 11:20-22).

Notice that Paul was upset because those who did not have as much were being humiliated by the freedoms of those who clearly could enjoy the luxury of fine dining at home in private. Paul was not rebuking the Corinthians because of their privileges and luxuries at home but because of their failure to commune with the less fortunate. Paul was preaching that the privileged ones needed no special treatment but that the ones in the body who did not have luxuries had to be included purposefully at the table of Communion lest they be left out. Paul's solution was not for the Corinthians to refrain from enjoying Communion and fellowship around the table. His solution was gracism through the art of inclusion. Notice what he wrote: "So then, my brothers, when you come together to eat, wait for each other. If anyone is hungry, he should eat at home, so that when you meet together it may not result in judgment" (1 Corinthians 11:33).

Discernment and inclusion are so important in the body of Christ that Paul would rather the more privileged folks eat at home before coming to the church fellowship dinner so that those with empty stomachs could feast on more of the community food. Now, that is a gracist thought worth pondering, isn't it?

It reminds me of the old argument about the weaker brother written about in 1 Corinthians 8, and the matters of conscience in Romans 14 about the eating of meat, as they relate to the modern-day arguments about Christians drinking alcohol. Paul's points are all consistent with one another. He was saying, if others are weaker, then choose to not enjoy your privilege around them in order that they may not be adversely affected. If you enjoy wine at home, go for it, but do not flaunt it in front of other Christians who may stumble over the thought of drinking alcohol. If you enjoy red meat but a vegetarian believes that meat eating is wrong for religious reasons, as was the case in the passages mentioned above, then enjoy the privilege of a juicy steak elsewhere.

The art of gracist inclusion means that I, as the stronger or privileged person, have the power and opportunity to give up my privilege in the face of those who do not have the privilege so that they may join with me, and me with them, in community. Valuing community and fellowship over comfort is a practical way to process Paul's statement about special treatment.

A PIECE OF PIE FOR THE OUTSIDERS

Remember the five visitors who didn't get any pie at the church dinner? How would a gracist in the group of fifty insiders act differently? A gracist in the majority group would either refuse the special treatment of having pie held back in the kitchen or would make certain that the outsiders were offered a piece of the pie before it was all gone. This is a clear example of looking out for those who don't have the privileged position or are on the fringes. Sharing the pie brings joy and fellowship to everyone.

Does this mean that special treatment is always wrong? No, not always. It is wrong only when it damages community, companionship or social mores. When my perks cause you pain or loss, then, like Paul said, "our presentable parts need no special treatment" (1 Corinthians 12:24). Do I want special treatment? Of course I do. My flesh loves the world and all its goodies. But the body is coordinated by the Spirit of God and not by the flesh. Therefore what I want and what I need are two distinct things. Do I need special treatment? No. Paul said the presentable parts—the majority persons, the insiders—do not "need" special treatment. In fact it is the visitor who needs the special treatment (gracism) so that he or she can partake in what others commonly enjoy. Paul's point is that I should be willing to share in your common experience for the sake of unity or be willing to lift you up to my status in order for us to share in community.

Refusing special favors in the face of others is a difficult concept to grasp because it seemingly argues against all I've earned and worked for. But please understand that I am not saying, nor do I believe Paul meant, that accomplishing and earning are wrong. There will always be different classes of people and various levels of status within churches and other communities. I believe, however, that gracism is the equalizer that will allow those of higher status to relate to those of lower status. The gracist who says, "I will share with you," is willing to sit in the home of a person whose home is not as nice for dinner instead of always hosting the meal. Sharing, beyond giving of what I have, can be the willingness to commune with others on their turf, at their home, in their part of the airplane. It can mean that I lay aside my prerogatives to enter another's reality.

Could Jesus not have availed himself of the accouterments of heaven when coming to earth? Sure, he could have. Yet Jesus chose to lay aside his divine prerogatives to dwell among mortals (Philippians 2:5-11). It was in that dwelling that fellowship and union took place. Jesus was willing to share in the commonality of our human experience. When was the last time you shared with someone in this way—shared in their experience, on their turf, in their world?

GRACE-ONOMICS

As a man I receive benefits and prerogatives that women do not. For example I can usually get a better deal when purchasing a vehicle than do many women. While this is not a universal rule, past studies have shown discrimination in the car sales industry when it comes to gender. So am I to refuse a good deal and pay more money for a vehicle than I have to in the name of gracism? No way. When my gracist nature must kick in, however, is when I know that a female friend is looking to purchase a vehicle. I should step alongside of her to ensure that she gets a good deal. Maybe I negotiate for her. Maybe on her behalf I call in one of my favors to a car dealer friend, ensuring that she receives the same treatment I was afforded. But I must do something. I cannot sit by and receive special treatment while she gets ripped off.

This kind of fight for justice must happen not simply on the personal level but systemically as well. When I become aware of others who are not being treated fairly while I'm being given special treatment, that should give pause inside of me to refuse my special status and make right what is wrong in a systemic way through advocacy for causes that defy injustice. Does gracism, as it relates to special treatment, prevent me from purchasing a nice home while others in the church live in trailers? Again, practically speaking, I cannot solve the financial gaps among people by purchasing homes for everyone in the church. I can, however, ensure that the person looking to buy a home is not being discriminated against when looking to get a bank loan for a new home. I can open doors to my network of loan officers and mortgage brokers who will bend over backward to do me a favor after my history of business with them.

I call this *grace-onomics*. It is the leveraging of financial and relational networks to help others succeed in their economic worlds. Assisting people in achieving financial success and reaching their educational and economic potential is a joy for me, especially when they may not have had the same opportunities, breaks or luck I have had. Grace-onomics are acts of gracism as they relate to money, class, opportunity and justice. Such acts are at the heart of reconciliation.

Whether church dinners, cars, homes, airline flights or other scenarios, the point is the same. There are those who are "unpresentable" (minorities, dotted, outsiders, on-the-fringe folks) who are in need of special treatment when I, the presentable one, am not. Therefore it is my Christian responsibility (which is different from my inalienable right as a human being) to refuse upgrades in the face of my brother or sister. I must either help the "unpresentable" ones to upgrade with me or share with them in their experience of lack. Otherwise I may get seduced by entitlements and become addicted to the prestige that comes with power—all of which can be gained on the backs or in the face of others who don't have the same insider information and networks that I've been afforded.

My friend Rick and I had a blast in economy class. Yes, we were crunched, but we shared in the experience—one of many crazy memories we enjoy. While Rick could have sat in business class, he chose community instead. Paul said that we were baptized by one Spirit and given one Spirit to drink (1 Corinthians 12:13). In this oneness we must figure out how we are to live together without one group putting down another while the other is elevated. The solution is gracism. A community of gracists is a group of believers who are crazy enough to believe that God's unifying Spirit is increasingly active among those who choose to lift each other up, cover one another and refuse special favors in the face of others who are on the fringes.

Gracist living doesn't refuse the good things that life has to offer. It simply refuses to ignore those who aren't as privileged to enjoy such benefits and is committed to doing something about it.

ANOTHER GRACIST MOMENT IN AN AIRPORT

I was traveling with a colleague named A. C. from the West to the East Coast with a stop in the Midwest. Instead of flying in economy class on this trip, I had the privilege of enjoying first class with my colleague. It was nice. However, we ran into a snag during our layover. While waiting in the Midwestern air-

port, A. C. and I went into one of the clubs for first-class travelers. I was without the proper plastic card that identified me as
someone who was allowed into the club. Because I was not on
the right air carrier for that particular club, we were not allowed
in the club.

The woman behind the counter apologized for the fact that
we would not be able to enter. Just then a gentleman by the
name of Chris who overheard the apology said, "They are with
me." The woman allowed us entry to the club as Chris's guests.
We didn't know Chris. He was a complete stranger to us. But
Chris was being a gracist to include two strangers so that we
could enjoy the accouterments of his club membership. Maybe
Chris (a white man) would have done this for anyone in the
same dilemma regardless of color. Who knows? All I know is
that A. C., a Latino male, and me as a black man, received kindness from a white guy in that moment. Whether this gentleman
was being a gracist or just an all-around nice guy, we were
thankful.

Later, while sitting in the club enjoying snacks with Chris,
we learned more. Through conversation we discovered that
Chris and I had actually heard of each other and had been
wanting to meet each other for a few years. A mutual friend of
ours named Clint had been telling us about each other and we
hadn't crossed paths until now. I discovered that the kind man's
full name was Chris Seay, a young pastor in Houston. Indeed
this man was a gracist. He was a Christian brother who noticed
that he had a privilege to share, and he included us in his spe-

cial space without giving it a second thought. It was clear that Chris's muscles of gracism had been regularly exercised. The gracist choice that Chris made was a second-nature reaction. His choice demonstrated that he had been living and breathing inclusion long enough that his decision was reflexive. Wouldn't it be great if our natural reflexes were to include instead of exclude? These kinds of in-the-moment responses can become normal for those who exercise gracist choices regularly.

The art of inclusion is the ability to reach out to those who are on the fringes. It is the extension of radical inclusivity to those who may not have the education, networks or breaks in life that I have had. It is inviting them in to enjoy the fruits of my world. Is this not what Jesus Christ did for us as our premier example of sharing?

REFLECTION QUESTIONS

1. Why do we struggle with the choices of community versus comfort? What are the benefits of each? What are the downsides of each?

2. When have you either benefited from or been excluded from "getting a piece of the pie"? When you are on the benefit side, how do you feel? What behaviors do you have to engage in? When you are on the excluded side, how do you feel? What behaviors do you engage in? How does receiving benefits or being excluded impact relationships?

3. Have you ever benefited from "grace-onomics"—the leveraging of financial and relational networks to help others suc-

ceed in their economic worlds? Are there people in your world whom you could help through grace-onomics? What are some of the reasons others might not have the financial and relational networks? What knowledge or skills would they need?

4. "Gracist living doesn't refuse the good things that life has to offer," the author says. "It simply refuses to ignore those who aren't as privileged to enjoy such benefits and is committed to doing something about it." What are three commitments you can make today that will help you be more of a gracist? Tell someone else the commitments you have made.

7

SAYING FOUR: "I WILL HONOR YOU"

(Greater Honor)

*God has combined the members of the body and has
given greater honor to the parts that lacked it.*

1 CORINTHIANS 12:24 (EMPHASIS ADDED)

Do you remember the mathematical equations you learned
in school that had symbols attached to them? Remember the
greater-than ($>$) and less-than ($<$) symbols? Once a number
was assigned to each side of the symbol, the elementary student was asked to choose which number was greater than or
less than the other. While I never really enjoyed mathematics,
I could achieve average scores with the greater-than and less-
than symbols.

Our heavenly Father values us all, but he is clearly a gracist
when it comes to his divine equations. Notice who Paul said
God honors when he combines people and assigns the greater-

than value of honor to people. Paul stated in 1 Corinthians
12:24 that "God has combined the members of the body and
has given greater honor to the parts that lacked it."

I find it unsettling to think that God would put a multicultural, multieconomical, multigifted and multidimensional
group of believers together and then assign a greater-than symbol to some of the people. Yet he does. Why? And to whom
does he assign the greater-than sign?

From Paul's statement it seems that God does not assign
greater honor to those with certain gifts, economic status or
even ethnicity, although some may argue that Paul was speaking of Gentiles here. It seems to me that the writer was clearly
stating that those who have "lacked it" (honor) are the ones
who have qualified for greater honor. Those groups who have
come with honor deficits are first in line for greater honor from
heaven's perspective.

THE FAIRNESS FACTOR

Do you know anyone who is honor deficient? These are people
who lack what the majority enjoy. People within the Christian
body and outside it who live in lack may qualify for honors they
did not earn if we follow Paul's logic in this passage. The normal
way of life for those in North America, generally speaking, is
one lived on the system of earnings, right? Basically, if one
works, one earns money. If one achieves, one is awarded. It is
that simple. If you do not achieve or work for your earnings,
then you fall short of honor and the normal rewards that come

with accomplishment. This seems fair and right.

The problem with grace is that it is unfair. Why should a homeless person or welfare recipient receive my hard-earned money if he or she chooses not to work? Have you ever thought this? I have. Admittedly this is not the most compassionate attitude, but at the same time the alarm on my fairness meter loudly sounds, "Unfair, unjust, foul." What about the work I've done? What about the investment of time, effort, energy, money, risk and faith it took for me to get to this level of life? What about the extra efforts I at times have had to make as an African American in the United States to overcome real and perceived odds?

Whenever I have found myself thinking like this, I have been reminded by the Spirit of God that I would be nothing if it were not for Christ. You have heard the saying "If not for the grace of God, there go I." That phrase settles the sounds of my fairness meter quickly. It takes only a few minutes of reflection on Psalm 103 to reorient me.

> The LORD is compassionate and gracious,
>   slow to anger, abounding in love.
> He will not always accuse,
>   nor will he harbor his anger forever;
> he does not treat us as our sins deserve
>   or repay us according to our iniquities.
> (Psalm 103:8-10)

The words above that say "he does not treat us as our sins de-

serve" are the ones that are etched into my mind. God really is
not fair. Grace is not fair. Theologians often argue for the justice
of God based on the death of Christ. In many ways I agree that
the justice requirement for our sin debt has been satisfied
through the substitutionary atonement of Jesus Christ. But that
still isn't fair. Justice may have been served, but Jesus still suf-
fered for sins he did not commit. While it is true that God the
Father is satisfied with the moral payment, do any of us believe
that Jesus got a fair deal?

I can't rejoice over the sufferings of Christ on my behalf. It
breaks me up. It makes me weep to think of the price my Savior
paid. My redemption was invaluable. Reflecting on it is evoking
an emotional response even as I write this line. It is not fair.
Jesus got a bum deal.

The reality is that we are all bums who have not earned one
thing we enjoy. If you have an education, it is because God
blessed you to get it. If you are smart and can think with a clear
mind, it is because God blessed you with a brain that works. If
you are athletic, the use of your limbs is a gift. The air we
breathe is a gift. When I begin to think like this, I am reminded
that, spiritually speaking, I was a beggar on the side of life's road
when Jesus gave me the bread of life to eat, living water to drink
and clothes of redemption to wear.

BANQUET AND BUMS

Jesus explained the concept of honor when he told the parable
of the banquet. The table of honor was occupied by those who

placed themselves at the most distinguished seats. Notice Jesus' advice for those who seek to be honored by others and not be self-promoting.

> When he noticed how the guests picked the places of honor at the table, he told them this parable: "When someone invites you to a wedding feast, do not take the place of honor, for a person more distinguished than you may have been invited. If so, the host who invited both of you will come and say to you, 'Give this man your seat.' Then, humiliated, you will have to take the least important place. But when you are invited, take the lowest place, so that when your host comes, he will say to you, 'Friend, move up to a better place.' Then you will be honored in the presence of all your fellow guests. For everyone who exalts himself will be humbled, and he who humbles himself will be exalted." (Luke 14:7-11)

God is in the exalting business and loves to honor his servants. He will give even greater honor to those who lack it most. When continuing to read Luke 14, we see that Jesus took the parable to another level as he explained the great wedding banquet. Because the invited ones (speaking of a majority of the Jewish people) rejected their invitation to salvation through Jesus Christ as the Messiah, the banquet host ordered his servants, "Go out quickly into the streets and alleys of the town and bring in the poor, the crippled, the blind and the lame" (Luke 14:21).

Who are the ones who lack honor and deserve a greater measure of it? In heaven's eyes it is the poor, crippled, blind and lame. That's right, the lower class, the outcast, the marginalized, the poor and disabled. It is these who have honor deficits that are made greater. The poor and the crippled are not going to walk into a prepared banquet. They must be sought after and retrieved. Greater honor is given to them by God. Initiation from the banquet hosts to search the streets for the less honorable is the representation of what God has done for each of us. You and I are the poor in spirit, the morally crippled, the spiritually blind and the emotionally lame people on the streets of sin and darkness. God, in his grace, has sent out the great host of heaven, Jesus Christ, and his servants to proclaim the good news that an undeserved banquet has been prepared. Unbelievable, isn't it?

Earlier I said that it is unsettling to me that God would extend greater honor to some. That is the effect of grace, though. It is unsettling and unfair and yet divine. I now believe it is okay to be unfair, not for the purposes of hurting others, but for the purposes of helping those who are in a state of lack. This kind of unfairness—gracism, if you will—is not only okay; it is commanded. Therefore, as a converted gracist, I must, like God, be an extender of grace and honor to everyone. Moreover, I must give greater honor to the ones who lack it most.

How? In four ways: service, speech, stewardship and sitting.

SERVICE

It honors God when I serve the poor, the crippled, the blind and the lame. When anyone has an honor deficit, regardless of color or class, it is my duty as a gracist to reach out and serve that person.

If you are a Puerto Rican, can you see yourself serving a Mexican? As American citizens, can we see ourselves serving immigrants? Even if we are against illegal immigration, when the human need for food, clothing or medical care confronts your community, are you willing to serve the human beings on your doorstep?

I remember when a vote came up on a foundation board that I served on. The vote was regarding donating money to an organization that would care for the human needs of Latinos in my community. A leader within the community had the calling and vision to minister to the human needs of Latinos and was requesting funds to do so. While deliberating the request, I had internal questions, as well as some open ones, about whether we were perpetuating illegal immigration by serving this foreign-born people group. Thinking personally about the people I have encountered, helped, related to and entertained in my home felt different to me than this decision. My personal care for human needs required one aspect of gracism, but now I was being asked to institutionalize the caring of foreign-born humans on a broader systemic basis.

After much consideration and thought I realized that without systemic change I could never impact greater numbers of people to receive the personal care that I afforded to a few. I now had the opportunity with one vote to help thousands of

Latinos regardless of their legal status. My conviction about the human need issue, whether legal or not, was solidified by Jesus' words to feed and care for the "least of these" (Matthew 25:40). In doing so we are doing it for Jesus himself. Whether the "least of these" came to America on slave ships from Africa, on rafts from Cuba or through the tunnels of Tijuana, I must have a heart to serve them personally and systemically. This is a way for me to practically honor those who are in lack.

SPEECH

When I speak in ways to lift up others who are beaten down by life and circumstances, even for those whose own choices placed them in the situation in which they find themselves, I honor them. Refusing to put people down who are already down-and-out is an honorable practice.

As a radio talk show host in Washington, D.C., I see and hear a lot of dishonoring communication in the name of Christianity. It breaks my heart to hear dishonoring speech that rips apart individuals and demonizes people in order to build up someone's political or spiritual view. I believe that good, honest and healthy debate is a great way to learn and challenge thinking. I'm all for debate. But when heated debate and disagreement turn into personal attacks, the demoralizing of opponents, character assassination and mean-spiritedness, I must draw the line. Even in disagreement our faith must guide us toward a no-tolerance policy for mean-spiritedness. I have witnessed mean-spirited speech on Christian radio shows where the host, callers and guests were debating politics, legalities and even Scripture passages (which I find ironic). If the basis for our debate is the Bible, then we are surely aware that God's Word never justifies mean-spirited or divisive speech.

One of the practical ways we as believers can honor others is through speech that is bridled and beneficial for the listener. We honor God and people by refraining from telling racial jokes that injure and verbal digs that degrade. When someone says something negative about a particular people group, we can open our mouths and offer an opposing example that is positive.

I remember a man stating how terrible Koreans were. He was an African American man in his fifties and he loathed the fact that Koreans were, as he put it, taking all the money from his community through their business practices. He referred to the Korean-owned grocery stores, liquor stores and cleaners in his community and said he resented them. He finished his tirade by saying, "I don't know one good Korean. Do you?"

I responded by asking him many questions publicly in this workshop of about forty people. I then told him that I knew many good Korean people, those who owned shops and those who didn't.

He pressed me publicly and said aloud, "Sure, Reverend, whatever you say. I bet you don't even know one good Korean. If so, then go ahead, name one. I'd like to meet him."

I retorted, "Then I would like to invite you to my home for dinner because my wife is Korean and she's lovely!"

After he picked up his jaw from the floor, he realized how callous his words were and fell back in his chair. The participants in the class laughed and cried. None of us will forget that workshop. The issue with this man wasn't the point he was making about Korean businesses but the lumping together of Koreans in a pejorative manner. Debating the matters related to businesses in the inner city is a discussion worth having, but the grouping of a nationality with negative descriptors and generalized language was inappropriate.

In such a racially tense world you will have many opportunities to balance callous words and dishonoring speech with opposing personal examples that are honoring and positive. Please take advantage of these opportunities.

STEWARDSHIP

When I invest time and money in programs and people who are about elevating those who lack honor in society, I'm sure that God is honored.

The reason I became a "big brother" to a thirteen-year-old African American boy whose parent is in the penitentiary and who lives in a small house with fourteen other relatives is because I realized that the children of inmates are at a disadvantage when it comes to achievement. Mentoring has been identified by research as one effective way of keeping kids moving in a productive direction that blesses the children and protects society.

The Amache program was started over five years ago by the

former mayor of Philadelphia, Dr. Wilson Goode. Mayor Goode was himself the child of an incarcerated father. His then pastor, along with the pastor's wife, took Wilson in as a young man to mentor him. Dr. Goode often speaks about how this intervention by loving adults changed the trajectory of his life. Dr. Goode went on to become the first African American mayor of Philadelphia. After his stint in office he was called into the gospel ministry as an ordained preacher before partnering with the Big Brothers/Big Sisters organization to start a mentoring program for children of incarcerated parents.

When I was asked to help Bridgeway Community Church join the program as a sponsoring church, and to become a mentor to a young teen myself, I knew that the cost of time and money would be significant. My commitment, if I chose to say yes to the mission, would be long term and not a one-time effort. I prayerfully agreed. We had a Father's Day service at Bridgeway shortly after I made my commitment and registered about eighty mentors for young boys and girls in our local area that Sunday.

Today I celebrated my little brother's fourteenth birthday with him. For his birthday we shopped for cool clothes, went out to lunch and then went to my house for chocolate cake that my wife had baked. Amber and the kids sang "Happy Birthday" and gave my little brother a card. After cake my little brother and I drove back to his house, where I dropped him off before coming here to Starbucks to rewrite this chapter. As I sit here I am struck by the fact that it has been an entire year of mentoring and I still feel like I have made only slow progress. It has taken months for my little brother to trust me, speak to me openly and relate in a way that resembles any kind of interdependence. I'm concerned about his fears, his friends and the gansta rap music he listens to (and repeats!). Yet I continue to spend time and money as an investment in him. I believe that my presence in his life will somehow make a difference. I honor my little brother who is lacking some of the basics I received growing up.

SITTING

When is the last time you sat with someone who lacked honor? Think of an AIDS patient, someone in rehabilitation or someone in a psych ward. Think of an invalid who moves slowly or an elderly person who simply wants to tell stories. In our fast-paced world the ministry of sitting with people may be the most powerful ministry of all.

By assigning greater-than values to the marginalized, the playing field of honor is leveled, God is pleased and everyone feels better. I spend a good amount of time sitting with people who I like and who are like me in meetings, in cars, on planes, at meals and in living room recliners. I mention this because I've become aware that there was a season in my life when I shielded myself from sitting with elderly people in need of conversation or visitation. I went way too long without visiting anyone in the hospital psych ward or prisoners. In realizing this I have become more proactive to exercise by sitting. I have worked out by sitting on park benches with the homeless, by making more hospital visits myself instead of sending someone else. I still have the calling to minister to those on the margins even if it doesn't fit neatly into my gift mix or personality preferences.

Isolation from a hurting world can be addictive. The intentionality of sitting is a discipline and a privilege. In the latest season of my life I have visited with the elderly, sat with my teenage little brother, traveled to funerals to be with the grieving, given to the homeless, listened to the depressed and psychologically challenged, called the lonely and extended kindness to those in need in some private ways. I share this not because I feel adequate in this area. Not by far. But I also know something about myself: if I am not intentional about reaching out to those who lack, I will slip into my private world of wealth, privilege and platform ministry in front of the masses. If I'm not careful, I can lose myself in the suburbs of my Christian faith and miss the "least of these." Jesus was intentional about not missing them, about not missing you and me.

Greater honor is given to those who lack it, according to God's Word. Therefore I must also assign greater honor to those who lack it within the body of Christ and beyond.

REFLECTION QUESTIONS

1. When does your fairness meter sound? Do you agree with the author that grace is unfair? How has God's being unfair benefited you?

2. Spend a quiet time in Psalm 103. List all the benefits God extends to us. Use that list in your prayer time with God, thanking him for his unfairness to you.

3. "I now believe it is okay to be unfair," the author states, "not for the purposes of hurting others, but for the purposes of helping those who are in a state of lack." Make a list of those in special need to whom our society extends grace (such as handicap parking). Why is the fairness factor with them not an issue?

4. What are some ways you can extend grace through service in your community?

5. When have you heard someone say something negative about a particular people group? What was your internal reaction? Did you respond to the people present there? If not you, did someone else? Write down a proactive response you can use at a future time when someone speaks negatively about a particular people group.

6. Of the four ways of extending grace—with my service, with my speech, with my stewardship, with my sitting—which one is the easiest for you to engage in? Which one is the hardest for you? Why?

8

SAYING FIVE: "I WILL STAND WITH YOU"

(No Division)

God has combined the members of the body and has given greater honor
to the parts that lacked it, so that there should be no division *in the body,*
but that its parts should have equal concern for each other.

1 CORINTHIANS 12:24-25 (EMPHASIS ADDED)

There are six things that God hates, according to Proverbs, and seven that are detestable to him. Dissension among brothers is the last item that elevates Solomon's list from six to seven (Proverbs 6:16-19). Throughout the Scriptures we find the same to be true. Division among believers is not of God. God hates division.

Whether in marriage, friendships, church ministries, denominations, ethnic groups, genders or families, what is it about division that assaults the very purpose and substance of God's desire for his people?

In the Garden of Eden division crept into the relationship between humankind and God because of the choice that Adam and Eve made to disobey God. The result was cataclysmic. The free will of humans—mixed with the temptation of the CEO of division himself, Satan—drove a wedge of separation between the Creator and his creation. The gospel message is that God so loved his created ones that he provided a way for the division to be mended through his Son, Jesus Christ, the CEO of unity.

God is one (Deuteronomy 6:4; John 10:30; 14:11; 17:22); he is totally unified in his triune divinity. God the Father, God the Son and God the Holy Spirit are three persons in perfect unity. If God is one in his nature and we are called to be one with him, then division and unity cannot be allowed to coexist among us.

John put it like this: "If anyone says, 'I love God,' yet hates his brother, he is a liar. For anyone who does not love his brother, whom he has seen, cannot love God, whom he has not seen. And he has given us this command: Whoever loves God must also love his brother" (1 John 4:20-21). In other words, because God is unified in his nature, he demands that those who follow him must reflect this unity in the body of Christ. Just as the human brain commands the rest of the human body, so Jesus Christ is the head of the spiritual body, the church, and commands the body to fall in line.

Therefore, when we cling to division, we align ourselves with the kingdom of darkness, led by Satan, the ultimate divider. Unity, on the other hand, aligns us with the God of unity and with Christ, the head of the church.

When community among believers is working right, there is nothing else as beautiful, nothing else as pleasant or divine. "How good and pleasant it is / when brothers live together in unity," declares the psalmist (Psalm 133:1).

MIGHTY PRAYERS

Praying together unifies people at the deepest level more than does any other spiritual practice I know. Praising God together is a close second. Prayer, however, brings us to our most humble place of dependence together.

The model prayer. Jesus taught a model prayer for his disciples to follow (Mathew 6:9-13). The first phrase of the prayer, "Our Father," identifies the commonality of our spiritual and familial relationship to God. We are part of one family as brothers and sisters in Christ. When brothers and sisters dwell together in unity, it honors God and blesses people.

While some measure of sibling rivalry is normal in families, as a dad, my heart is broken whenever my children fight with each other. I want the family to be in unity and to not be at odds with each other. Disagreements are okay, but when discussion turns into words of anger and hate, I am dismayed and begin the discipline process if agreement and forgiveness don't soon transpire. I can only imagine what our heavenly Father must feel when his children are at odds with one another. When we reaffirm in prayer that we are, indeed, children of our heavenly Father, this reminds us of our spiritual connection and responsibilities as family members.

The Master's prayer. The longest prayer of Jesus recorded in Scripture is for the oneness of his offspring. God hates it when his children fight even more than I hate it for my children. This is why Jesus prayed for the oneness of his disciples. Jesus interceded on behalf of his disciples and all those who would come to faith through their message, which includes all of us in the twenty-first century (John 17). When I write "all of us," this means Christians throughout the entire world in this century regardless of region or affiliation. Arab Christians are just as much our Christian family members as Canadian or American, Pakistani or Indian Christians. If we are praying "Our Father," we are affirming our family connection like Jesus was when he prayed to our Father about unity. The Master's prayer confirms his desire for his brothers and sisters to stop fighting and start affirming their common bloodline in Christ.

The martyr's prayer. Jesus' time in the Garden of Gethsemane before his death was emotional and spiritual. After sharing with the Father his desire not to be crucified, Jesus came to a deep resolve in his heart and mind. He said to God the Father, "Yet not as I will, but as you will" (Mathew 26:39). While Jesus may have been divided in his emotions, he submitted his will to the Father's will for the purpose of regaining oneness among humankind and God, reversing the effects of division born in the Garden of Eden.

The model prayer begins with "Our Father" and continues to focus on God's purpose in the first half of the prayer. Indeed the prayer can easily be viewed in halves. The first half is a prayer to the Father about himself and his purposes (Matthew 6:9-10). The second half of the prayer is addressed to the Father about us as humans and our needs (verses 11-13). Below I have quoted the first half of the prayer. Pay special attention to how Jesus ended this half.

> Our Father in heaven,
>   hallowed be your name,
> your kingdom come,
> your will be done
>   on earth as it is in heaven. (Matthew 6:9-10)

Did you see the connection? Jesus taught in his model prayer that we are to pray for God's will to be done, just as he would later do in the Garden of Gethsemane. This begs a question about God's will. While we all have our own volition, as seen in the first garden where humans originally sinned, leading to separation from God, Jesus taught and modeled for us submission to the will of God. In both prayers, the model and martyr's prayers, Jesus demonstrated the priority of God's will on earth. The model prayer doesn't simply pray for God's will but specifies what that will is and where it is to happen, namely "on earth as it is in heaven."

MULTICULTURAL PRAISE

In order for us to know what God's will on earth is "as it is in heaven," we must get a picture of heaven. Allow the passage below to paint the picture better than my words could. The believers in heaven sang a new song:

> You are worthy to take the scroll
>   and to open its seals,
> because you were slain,
>   and with your blood you purchased men for God
>   from every tribe and language and people and nation.
> You have made them to be a kingdom and priests to
>   serve our God,
>   and they will reign on the earth. (Revelation 5:9-10)

In a loud voice they sang:

> "Worthy is the Lamb, who was slain,
> to receive power and wealth and wisdom and strength
> and honor and glory and praise!" (Revelation 5:12)

> After this I looked and there before me was a great multitude that no one could count, from every nation, tribe, people and language, standing before the throne and in front of the Lamb. (Revelation 7:9)

Jesus was the Lamb of God who was slain by humans whom he purchased with his blood. The population of the redeemed in heaven are racially, ethnically and nationally diverse. How beautiful! Do you see why Jesus' model prayer and martyr's prayer are connected regarding God's will? The will of God is that all of the redeemed would be one on earth as it is, and will be, in heaven.

Does your will conform to the will of God? We can choose

division, as was true of the first Adam in the first garden, or submission, as was true of the second Adam in the second garden (Romans 5:12-17). God's will is that we, as his children, are unified in love and worship on earth as in heaven.

The model and martyr's prayers were bridged by the Master's prayer for unity in John 17. Jesus prayed that the unity of believers would be complete so that the world would know the love of God by witnessing it. "May they be brought to complete unity to let the world know that you sent me and have loved them even as you have loved me," Jesus pleaded (John 17:23).

What a mighty connection among the three prayers of Jesus! Division on any basis is not an option for Jesus' church. If Jesus was concerned about it and had to pray for it, how much more should we pray for it? God's desire is for his church to be a "house of prayer for *all* nations" (Isaiah 56:7, emphasis added).

STANDING TOGETHER

The diversities of giftedness, gender, race, class, perspectives and preferences may collide and even compete at times. Grace within relationships then becomes the oil that keeps the body working together toward the goal of unity while fending off division within the body of Christ.

It is in this vein that the next saying—"I will stand with you"—emerges. In 1 Corinthians 12:24 Paul said, "God has combined the members of the body and has given greater honor to the parts that lacked it," as we discussed in the last chapter. Notice the verse that follows: " . . . so that there should be no division in the body." Did you catch it? When we don't assign greater honor to those who lack it, the door of division is thrown wide open.

Those who lack honor may over time become resentful, angry or even bitter if they feel continually walked on, overlooked, underappreciated, underpaid or discriminated against. If the undervalued are not given honor, they may rise up to fight for honor. This may come through speech, attitude, politics, complaining, conniving or even violence.

I will never forget the conversation I had with former congressman, pastor and civil rights leader the Reverend Walter Fauntroy. He explained to me, when discussing his role in the life of Dr. Martin Luther King Jr. as a social activist and civil rights organizer, how those who are disenfranchised and discriminated against begin to feel embittered toward the powers that be. The pain of their powerlessness and invisibility mounts up into volcanic anger toward those who live safe and secure lives. If it is perceived that the "haves" are the cause of some people being "have-nots," then the "have-nots" become embittered toward the "haves." More crassly put, Fauntroy said that if those who have don't share with those who don't, then it will be only a matter of time before those who don't have will try to violently take it. Whether or not such an extreme of force and violence is true, can you see the point of frustration and division that can be wedged between the "haves" and the "have-nots," between the powerful and the powerless?

Paul addressed the dilemma of division that could potentially cause a breach within the body. He offered an answer that will prevent division, namely giving greater honor to those who are deficient of it. Don't ignore them; exalt them. Honor them. Help them. Lift them up. Use your power to encourage, inspire, protect and bring them into the fold. In so doing you will fend off the thing that God hates—division. Racism, discrimination, segregation and classism divide, but gracism unites. Gracism heals.

Just to be clear, I am not advocating rewarding criminal behavior or enabling laziness. I am encouraging a heart attitude that seeks to bless first and judge second. We must seek to comprehend the pain that causes deviance rather than simply dismissing the "have-nots."

SAVE THE RHINOS

The television news show *60 Minutes,* with Dan Rather, reported on white rhinos in South Africa. While the white rhino population is a protected species, the news story reported that they were being killed off one by one. There was a season when 10 percent of the white rhino population was being hunted. Game park rangers were unsure of what was happening since there was no evidence from the dead rhino carcasses of poachers or hunters. After investigation a shocking discovery was made. As hard as it was to believe, rangers discovered that teenage elephants were killing the rhinos. It was very unusual for elephants to be predators. Rangers began to tag the elephants and document their behavior through surveillance. Like having a criminal rap sheet on each of the elephants, it was documented that a group of adolescent elephants were the culprits.

Why would teenage elephants become predatory bullies acting as juvenile delinquents? The answer went back fifteen to twenty years. Because of the overpopulation of elephants in South Africa, much like deer in my part of the country, there was an official choice made to kill the adult elephants and relocate the baby elephants by airlifting them to another part of the country. After a decade of growing up in the wild without the adult elephants as an influence, the younger elephants had no guidance as to what was right and wrong. The younger elephants grew up without anyone teaching them that killing rhinos was inappropriate behavior for elephants.

Seeking a solution that would not involve killing the delinquent elephants, the rangers made a corrective decision they hoped would solve the problem. The officials airlifted a group of adult elephants to the wildlife area where the younger delinquents lived. Within a short period of time, the older elephants reestablished order and authority. The killing ended. What an amazing documentary! When I watched it, I was moved because I realized that God has established order even within the animal kingdom. In addition the story speaks to so many of our social issues—mentoring, crime, security, authority, community and even the role of the elderly in our multigenerational society. Because the delinquents had no role models, they ran rampant and brought disorder to the environment, harming the preserved species.

Had there been no one to stand for the white rhinos, maybe they would be extinct in South Africa now. Figuratively speaking, who is standing up for the white rhinos in your family or neighborhood? Who is standing for the rhinos in our country, in our cities or in our congregations? Maybe you feel like a white rhino who is in an unsafe environment and you feel helpless. You deeply desire for someone with the resources to stand with you, to stand up for you. Whoever the white rhinos are in any given sociological environment, they need protection from harmful elephants. Whether the harm is intentional or unintentional, natural or unnatural, intervention is necessary to solve the problem.

Imagine how the heart of God is warmed when his children get along in peace. Elephants and rhinos living together in safety is better than killing and death, right? Once safety and value are established, then community and communion have a chance. Imagine what heaven must feel when all of God's children in Christ dwell together in unity.

What a wonderful answer to Jesus' prayer when you and I put aside our differences and choose to stand together! Moreover what a unifying goal when you and I stand together to give greater honor to those in our community who are lacking it! It unifies us when we have a common goal to elevate, protect and preserve the lowly among us, whoever they are—whether rhinos, young or old elephants, or officials making choices that affect the entire society.

A CHALLENGING STAND

A few months ago I led a group of believers to the Holy Land for a tour. On one of our days in Israel our group got off the well-worn path of other tourists and took the plunge into a Palestinian territory, where we shopped and interacted with the locals. Because our Jewish guide was not allowed behind the wall that contained the Palestinian people, we were left in the care of a Muslim Palestinian driver and a Christian Palestinian guide who joined our group to explain the lay of the land.

While shopping and viewing different sites, I conducted several interviews with the locals about the Palestinian-Israeli conflict. One man I interviewed was the Palestinian Christian who was guiding us. I will call him Ahmed. I asked Ahmed questions about his life, faith, politics and affiliations. His passions bled through everything he said. Curious about the mix between being a Palestinian and a Christian, I asked Ahmed to explain his life as a Palestinian Christian. He said, "David, we Christian Palestinians don't fit in anywhere. As a Christian, the Muslims reject us. As a Palestinian, the Jews reject us. We often feel isolated and alone in our struggle to live in the Middle East as Christians and as Palestinians."

When asked how he reconciles his faith with the social ills he is forced to live with, he began to break out of his well-crafted English with a Middle Eastern accent to a fast-paced English with a heavy Arab accent. His emotion took over. "Admittedly," he said, "I confess that it is very difficult for us as a people to live under these conditions of oppression from the Israeli government. Many of us Palestinians feel caged in and angry about the injustices we face through the system that is in place." Having to live a life of lack within the confines of a cement wall, or travel through the humiliation of an Israeli checkpoint by day and under the fear of Muslim warlords who take to the streets by night, has put many people in a state of hopelessness. The interview had a profound effect on me. I chose to return two months later with a friend to learn more so that I could stand with and for the Palestinian people. A part of that commitment is to expose their plight and make others aware of the tragedies the West seldom hears about.

A JEWISH GRACIST

An old Jewish friend of mine named Leo advocates for the plight of the Palestinians and is as passionate for bridge building as I am. Leo asked me, while sitting at his dining room table, "What are your people, the Christians, going to do about the plight of the Palestinians?" I was speechless. He pressed further to argue that my religion, Christianity, was supposed to be one of love and concern for the poor and the suffering. Yet he sees Christians standing with Jews, his people, who by and large don't believe in Jesus Christ as the Messiah. Leo went on to say, "My religion, Judaism, clearly states in the Torah that the stranger is to be treated well." In Leo's opinion the Jews were not even following their own laws from the Torah. Standing with the Palestinians who are suffering under poverty, Islamic extremism and the military oppression of the Jewish government, Leo is challenging Christians, Jews and Muslims to stand up for the oppressed Palestinians. He even argued before Congress on behalf of the Palestinians, only to receive ridicule from his own community. Though he hadn't heard the term before, Leo was acting as a gracist. He would simply call himself a good Jew.

I've spoken to Jewish friends and Israeli officials about the plight of the Palestinians. Many of them are perplexed by the unfortunate scenario in Israel. There is definitely a need for Israel's security in a neighborhood where many want them to be deleted from existence. The other side of the despicable coin is the victimization of the Palestinian people who under the thumb of harsh military actions are often humiliated every day at checkpoints and in their poverty-stricken conditions. My point is simply this: let's balance our prayers for the peace of Israel with prayers for the plight of the Palestinians. God cares for them both, as should we. Gracism demands it.

Standing with and for others who are the "least of these" is not a popular position, but it is one that Jesus commends to us so that love will penetrate the human heart and division among enemies will be healed. While it is not a natural human instinct to gravitate toward the least, lonely, last and left out, it is godly. Standing with those on the fringes comes from a heart that is concerned for others. The resulting benefit will hopefully minimize division and maximize unity.

HOW DO I SIGN UP FOR THIS?

Practically speaking, how can we live out the "I will stand with you" saying? When you and I agree to stand with and for the disenfranchised, we are being gracists. We are standing in the gap for those who may not be able to speak for themselves. And many times, even when they do speak, they are not heard. You and I have friends and networks, political connections, board contacts and sometimes simply a hand of invitation to the table of feasting that can be a gesture of standing with someone on the fringes.

Standing with people sometimes means standing up for people. My goal in this book has been to press the principles of gracism into our hearts and minds with the hopes that God will show you and me practical ways to apply these principles when the opportunity presents itself in your context. I believe that God always gives us opportunities to apply what we learn. My prayer is that God will show you your open door of opportunity to be a gracist in some way today or this week.

There are times when much more may be required of a gracist. In times of overt discrimination, or covert racism and injustice, it may be required of you and me to stand up for the rights of those whose voices have been muted by the powers that be. You may find yourself in the halls of Congress speaking up for the voiceless, on the streets of your city marching for a cause, in the ballot booth of your local school voting for a candidate who will serve the disenfranchised or simply in the choir director's office speaking for a choir member in the church who is not getting an opportunity to sing like others. The principle is the same. Stand up for the needy. Speak up for the voiceless. Rise up for those whose wings are clipped. Stand!

STANDING BY GRACE

Jesus quoted from the prophet Isaiah when he publicly read,

> The Spirit of the Lord is on me,
>> because he has anointed me
>> to preach good news to the poor.
> He has sent me to proclaim freedom for the prisoners
>> and recovery of sight for the blind,
> to release the oppressed,
>> to proclaim the year of the Lord's favor. (Luke 4:18-19)

After closing the scroll from which he read in the synagogue, Jesus exclaimed, "Today this scripture is fulfilled in your hearing" (Luke 4:21).

This must have freaked out the religious leaders of the day, who were used to smug piety and clerical segregation from the commoners. Jesus was a gracist. He reached out to the poor and the prisoners, the disabled and the oppressed, so that they would not be divided from him or us. You and I can stand only because of his grace. None of us would have a thing were it not for the grace of God in our lives. If God were not a gracist, you and I would have no power, no pleasure, no purpose and no possessions. If you have the ability to read this sentence, you have been graced. Therefore for any of us to ever feel justified in being elitist, arrogant or cocky in any way would be absurd, wouldn't it? If not for grace, we would still be marginalized on the fringes of salvation awaiting eternal judgment. There is no room for boasting about gifts, talents, capabilities, abilities, heritage, race or ethnicity. Paul knew firsthand of such temptation. When evaluating his religiosity through circumcision, nationalism through Israel, tribalism through Benjamin, ethnocentrism as a Hebrew of Hebrews and elitism through Pharisaical status, Paul counted it all as garbage compared to gaining salvation through Jesus Christ and the surpassing greatness of knowing him intimately (Philippians 3:5-9).

When Paul wrote the striking fact "It is by grace you have been saved, through faith—and this not from yourselves, it is the gift of God—not by works, so that no one can boast" (Ephesians 2:8-9), he was talking about himself, the early Christians and us. The propensity to forget that we are saved and sustained by grace (God's ridiculous favor) is overwhelmingly natural. To be reminded of the grace it took to save us is exactly the pride adjustment I need whenever I get too big for my britches.

The special grace of God keeps us levelheaded and reminds us that we are all one in Christ. We are all redeemed by grace regardless of our distinction. How ridiculous it would be to separate over these very distinctions! Therefore, since Christ stood in the gap for you and me, will you now have that same attitude to stand with and for others? Not as their savior but because of the Savior. If we will do this, the forces of division will be thwarted among believers. Will you say to others on the fringes, "I will stand with you when you are mistreated, devalued, ignored or left out"? I believe that when choruses of believers sing this phrase "I will stand with you" with passion and conviction for one another, true unity will abound. Otherwise the result will be the dissension and division God hates.

REFLECTION QUESTIONS

1. How have you experienced the pain of division or conflict that led you and another, or you and a group, from continuing to be a part of each other's lives? What are some of the emotions that are stirred from that separation as you reflect on it today? What were the consequences of that division?

2. When have you experienced unity with another person or group of people? What emotions do you feel when strongly connected to others? What are the results that have come from the experience of unity for you, others, a church or a group?

3. Read all three prayers of Jesus (Matthew 6:9-13; 26:39, 42; John 17). Write down the words and phrases from each prayer that you are especially drawn to. Read Revelation 5:6-14 and write down the words and phrases from that passage that you are drawn to. How are the lists from the passages different? How are they similar?

4. What was your response to the story in this chapter about the Palestinian Christians? How does your view of history, politics or race impact your reaction to the needs of this group of Christians?

9

SAYING SIX: "I WILL CONSIDER YOU"

(Equal Concern)

God has combined the members of the body and has given

greater honor to the parts that lacked it,

so that there should be no division in the body,

but that its parts should have equal concern for each other.

1 CORINTHIANS 12:24-25 (EMPHASIS ADDED)

Have you ever driven through a major city and come to a stoplight where there was a homeless person limping toward your car seeking a handout? Or maybe you have taken a walk down an urban street or visited a tourist area only to be confronted by someone who gave you a sad story of his need for money to catch a bus or get something to eat. How does it make you feel when that happens to you?

Would anyone reading this book be honest enough to confess that there are times when you have wanted to cross the street before the homeless person approached you? Have you ever hoped that the light would turn green before the moment of decision faced you, easing your conscience?

This has happened to me on multiple occasions. It is never easy to watch someone who is poor or downtrodden struggle. Being on the frontline of poverty is disconcerting, to say the least. Moreover it is tempting to be judgmental about the motives of the homeless one. We surmise that she will buy drugs or alcohol with the money we give her. We excuse our inaction with our busy schedules, not having time to stop and give money, food or even a look of dignity to those "bums."

THE OTHER SIDE

What would Jesus do in this kind of situation? He explained it in his own words (Luke 10:30-37).

Jesus told the story of man who was lying on the side of the road, having been beaten by robbers and left for dead. A priest witnessed the man's downtrodden state and yet crossed the road and walked down the other side of the street without helping him. After the priest got as far from the helpless man as possible, a Levite (another kind of religious leader of the day) also passed by the man who had been mugged. Like the priest, the Levite passed by on the other side of the road to avoid contact with the man, absolving himself of responsibility and leaving the victim for someone else to help.

Finally, a third man encountered the downtrodden soul lying on the ground. This man was a Samaritan, one who was racially mixed with Jewish blood. The Samaritan took pity on the man. His concern for the hurt man drove him to action. He bandaged the victim's wounds, pouring oil and wine on him. He then picked up the man and placed him on his donkey, escorting him to a local inn, where he invested his own resources to assure that the victim's stay was paid for.

THREE LOVING ACTS OF GRACE

The Samaritan did three loving things that underscored the point about loving one's neighbor that Jesus was teaching through this parable. First, the Samaritan "took pity" on the downtrodden man (Luke 10:33). This means he had a *merciful heart*. Second, the Samaritan took action by bandaging the man's wounds and escorting him to a safe place where he could heal. This demonstrates a *shepherding heart*. The third act of love by the Samaritan was to invest in the healing of the victim by paying the innkeeper for the time spent in the inn, offering additional money if the man needed to stay longer. The Samaritan showed a *generous heart* as he gave of his finances.

When we see the condition of the Samaritan's heart, we aren't looking for spiritual gifts of mercy, shepherding and giving. We are seeing a transformed heart that beats the way Jesus' heart would beat. Beyond giftedness is graciousness. It's a heart thing.

When we encounter people from the "other side," what are we to do? Jesus taught us to love them with active compassion. The heart attitudes of the first two characters focused only on how to avoid the problem, while the third character engaged the problem as an opportunity to love. A concerned heart should lead to compassionate actions. What is our heart like? Is it a heart that seeks to avoid those in need or one that engages the problem as an opportunity to love?

Unfortunately the religious leaders were more focused on their beliefs than on living out their faith through loving actions. This is the heart of eternal life. Jesus said, "Do this and you will live" (Luke 10:28). Eternal life is found in God's love for us and our love for God. It is a relationship of love and response. Such vibrancy in a true relationship of intimacy with God will overflow into our human relationships and acts of compassion. How could it not? When you have been touched by God's compassion and mercy, it would be scandalous to not be compassionate and merciful to others. A heart that is eternally alive beats with the rhythms of mercy, shepherding care and generosity.

The priest and the Levite were too concerned about themselves, their schedules, status and other preoccupations, to see the point that Jesus was making in the parable, namely that love and compassion take action. The recipients of the action are those in need, those who are hurting, downtrodden and on the edges of our normal social networks.

How are you doing with such gracist acts of outreach in our world of seemingly greater isolation and guardedness from those who are on the fringes of society? Isn't it curious to you that these are exactly the ones with whom Jesus hung out? He was always mixing it up with sinners, tax collectors, prostitutes, the blind and hungry. What is that all about? Jesus had a merciful and concerned heart; what about us?

GETTING BACK ON THE RIGHT SIDE OF THE STREET

Even as I am writing this page I am feeling the conviction of God's Spirit. I confess to you that I'm not gracist enough. I seek isolation and protection from the ills of society, which includes the people who go with those ills. These are the people whom Christ was seeking to hang out with and touch. Yet in my world of cul-de-sac living, garage door closing, back deck relaxing and mountaintop retreating, I can easily shut out the undesirable people whose pain is too much for me to bear. Would you pause with me for a prayer of confession and forgiveness?

Dear Lord, please forgive me for my insensitivities toward the hurting and downtrodden. Please forgive me for acting like the priest and Levite more often than the Samaritan. Help me to be more gracist in my life, more concerned. Father, I thank you for your grace, mercy and compassion on me. Thank you for not leaving me on the side of the road. Help me to extend that kind of love to more people in my world. I pray in Jesus' name, amen.

I WILL CONSIDER YOU

How can we have "equal concern" like Paul spoke of in 1 Corinthians 12:24-25? Do you remember what he said? "God has combined the members of the body and has given greater honor to the parts that lacked it, so that there should be no division in the body, but that its parts should have *equal concern* for each other."

Self-preoccupation can keep Christians from experiencing the multicultural, multiracial and multidenominational unity God desires for us. When Christians stop reacting negatively to sociopolitical terminology like *affirmative action, special interest* or *equal opportunity,* and instead use Paul's terms *special honor, greater honor* and *equal concern,* it will change our attitudes from a "me and mine" to a "we and ours" mentality. Instead of holding on to the attitudes of the priest and Levite, let's cling to the Samaritan's merciful heart. Jesus said, "Go and do likewise" (Luke 10:37).

The sixth saying of a gracist is "I will consider you." I will concern myself with your feelings and your dreams whether I'm walking down the street like the good Samaritan or in the halls of Congress voting for the things that concern you.

EQUAL CONCERN

The term Paul used for equal concern literally means "same care" and has the idea of possessing an anxious interest at the same level that I would have for myself or one I love.

Equal concern begs the question, equal to whom? Paul said that we should have equal concern for each other. I should be thinking about your interest and you should be thinking about mine. This means that I am to consider your thoughts, perspectives and feelings rather than making a unilateral decision that might adversely affect you. There is not one group that should be ignored or passed over. All should be included if possible and considered always. Gracists consider the concerns of others who are not like them, those in a different giftedness, color, gender, educational or class category. Would there not be less church division if people were bent on radical inclusivity and made it a normal practice to pause in consideration of other's feelings and perspectives? Boy, wouldn't marriages be happier if spouses employed the equal-concern principle of gracism with each other? Wouldn't relationships soar if gracism were rampant?

THEM AND US?

Paul was saying that there should not be a "them versus us" mentality in the body of Christ. My concern for "them" should be just as deep as my concern for "us." I was broadened in my thinking about this when I engaged in an intellectually stimulating conversation for several hours with former President Bill Clinton about race relations along with a small group of religious leaders. When asked about racial reconciliation and its importance, President Clinton told a story of growing up in Arkansas in a single-parent household where neighbors were repeatedly invited over. He said that it is natural to have a "them versus us" mentality until people are invited into your home. At that point the people who were known as "them" became the "us" by virtue of the fact that they were in our home regularly. Houseguests are no longer "those people" across the street but they are a part of "us." We are them and they are us. Furthering the discussion he said (I am paraphrasing), "If something negative or unfortunate happened to our neighbors who lived across the street who we had over continually, it was as if it were happening to us because they were 'us.' "

I realized then, and still believe now, that the "them versus us" mentality plagues race relations, denominational distinctions and cultural differences to such a degree that it is hard for compassion to cross over to the other side of the street. If I don't see the man lying on the side of the road as one who is a part of my family, ethnicity, religious group or class, then it is easier to dismiss him.

Jesus so loved the world that he bridged the gap between humanity and heaven by becoming like us and empowering us to become like him. When we begin to see people of different backgrounds as "us" and not as "them," we will be able to minister compassion and mercy at deeper levels of identification. When we see the victimized man on the side of the road, we must not see him as a stranger but as a brother in our family of humanity who needs our concern.

The phrase "equal concern" (or anxious interest) from 1 Corinthians 12:25 is the same terminology Paul used in 2 Corinthians 11:28 when he said, "Besides everything else, I face daily the pressure of my concern for all the churches." Notice Paul's concern for all the churches. He had anxious interest and varying concerns about all the churches under his apostleship. It was the same kind of concern that a parent has for multiple children. I don't know of one parent who wishes for the success of one child while desiring for another child to fail. Conversely, while the path of success for each child is different, the parent's interest in the success of each child is equally fervent.

Paul was saying that we are all one; we are all connected in one body, the church, with one head of that body, Jesus Christ. Therefore we must have equal concern for one another regardless of our distinctions. There is no "them" and "us" in the body of Christ. And on a broader human scale the distinctions between unredeemed and redeemed humans are not as vastly different as we might think. We may not all be the same in our redemptive status, but we all have the potential to be since Jesus Christ died for all humans and not just for one class or race of people. Therefore I must view every person not from a worldly viewpoint but from a spiritual point of view where I see them as Jesus Christ sees them (2 Corinthians 5:16).

A KOREAN CHURCH MOVE

While I was presenting a workshop to several pastors in California, a man asked a question about a move that his church was planning to make to the city. He wanted to know what I thought about the fact that his all-Korean church had purchased a piece of land in an area of the inner city that had a majority population of poor African Americans and Hispanics. The young pastor's concern was that his large Korean congregation was going to commute into the city on Sundays for church and then retreat to the suburbs after services. Because the services would be conducted in Korean, and many of those in the Korean community were not interested in building crosscultural relationships (according to this pastor), he wondered what effect such a move would have on those in the city. What a thoughtful question!

This is exactly what I mean by a gracist saying, "I will consider you," before making drastic moves and big decisions. Questions about the impact on a community, a ministry, an ethnic group, a class, a neighborhood, a corporation or a department are all gracist questions that help us to consider the impact of our choices.

I affirmed the Korean brother who asked for my opinion about the Korean church moving into the urban community. I recommended ways he could build a bridge to the urban community through an English-speaking outreach ministry. He was receptive to and enlightened by the ideas. Other thoughts about how to minister to the community through initiatives that would serve the population at large would aid the Korean church in building bridges with its neighbors and fulfilling the Great Commission at the same time. I was blessed by his consideration of the impact his church's move would have on the community.

BUM ON THE BENCH IN BALTIMORE

It was a beautiful day in Baltimore when the American Regatta boats were visiting the Baltimore Harbor. The event was a gala that had been planned for VIPs such as the mayor, the governor, the head coach of the Baltimore Ravens football team, the business elite and other movers and shakers from the city. This gathering was replete with a spread of food, drinks and entertainment by the harbor next to the world-famous boats. I was fortunate enough to be invited by a friend to attend the event to schmooze and network. I had a blast at the gathering. But the highlight of the evening came when I decided to take a walk along the harbor to take a breather from the crowd and reflect on the evening. While walking I came across a homeless man who was sitting on a bench observing the ritzy crowd, listening to the music and smelling the food. While strolling along in my suit and tie, I greeted the man with a casual hello. He returned the greeting. Then I felt a clear prompting in my spirit to go toward the man. I asked him if I could sit down on the bench next to him. He agreed.

Picture two black men sitting on a harbor bench and looking out over the water with a crowd of people about a hundred feet away sipping drinks and eating hors d'oeuvres. As we peered out we began to chat.

"My name is David," I said. "What's yours?"

"Harvey," he responded.

"Nice to meet you, Harvey."

Once we got passed our introductory chatter, I asked a more penetrating question. "You live on the streets?"

"Yep, the streets are my home," he said.

"Why is that? What makes a man like you homeless?"

Harvey explained that he used to be a professional worker in

Pennsylvania but suddenly lost his job, followed by the loss of his marriage and family. Harvey explained that he went through some really hard times. After I had listened to his story, we discussed his lack of health care and his current living situation. Harvey definitely had opinions about politics, the gala he was watching, homelessness and other social issues.

Harvey said, "The streets are my home now, and my family and friends are here now." He explained the community of friendship among the homeless. He also told me of his time in different shelters and what life on the streets was like. "The shelters are okay. At least you can get a bed and meal if you need it, but you have to stay around to listen to the church folk as a part of the deal."

Toward the end of the hour-long conversation we came to the point where it was time to depart. I gave Harvey my number in case he ever wanted to call me. I offered other kinds of help if he wanted it.

"Honestly, Dave," Harvey said, "just the fact that you sat down and talked with me was all I needed. God bless you, bro."

I felt like I gave dignity to Harvey that evening while he was sitting on the sidelines of a dignified event. While I know that I must consider people like Harvey more often, I can honestly say that on that day I considered someone purely out of goodness and not to receive anything in return. The funny thing about this is that I walked away feeling more blessed than when I sat down. Out of all of the business cards I passed out that night, Harvey's phone call from a public pay phone or shelter was the only one I was really looking forward to receiving. My harborside conversation with him was the best conversation I had all night. To date I've not heard from Harvey, but maybe I'll run into him on the dock again sometime.

We follow the model of Jesus when we reach out to the margins, whether on the streets or in the church. As he conveyed in the good Samaritan story, the Lord desires for us to be compassionate people, caring people and contributors to the lives and well-being of others. That is what it means to have equal concern.

One of the small things I've integrated into my life since meeting Harvey is keeping coins in my car door. Each time I break a dollar and receive change back from a cashier, I put the change in my car door pocket so that I'm always prepared to give change to those who come up to my window. I know it's a small thing, but it reminds me that I'm connected to a broader human story. It is a gracism moment that God uses as a reminder for me and hopefully a blessing to a homeless person.

CONSIDERING AFRICA

For every time I have been considerate I can think of two times when I have failed to consider others in proper ways. I am working hard on living out the book I am writing. Just when I thought I was doing well, I received a letter from a church attender who was upset about my referring to Africa when speaking about real poverty. At first this may not seem like a big deal, but after reading her letter and seeing it from her perspective, it makes complete sense.

Dear Pastor Anderson,

Thank you for your ministry. I really enjoy attending Bridgeway and the multicultural ministry here. However, I had a very difficult time listening to your message on wealth when you referred to Africa and poverty. I was offended by you saying that you never saw real poverty until you went to Africa. You see, Africa is usually thought of, by many Americans, as one country. Africa is thought of as just one place where people are running around poor, in war and living in horrific conditions. However, Africa is a continent with over fifty countries. These countries each have their own governments, people and cultures. Just like the U.S. and other countries, there are both urban and rural places in African countries.

Therefore, generalizing the whole continent is a big mistake that has several negative repercussions. The media, which is obviously very influential on people's ideas, tends to focus mainly on the poor, rural, diseased or war-torn places. In fact I am from an African country and have had people come to me and ask me questions like "So, are you going back to the war?" Then I have to explain to them that I will be going back home and that the country I am from in Africa is not experiencing any war. Other questions and comments I have heard are "Oh, thank God you were rescued from that place," "Did you wear clothes before you got here?" and "Had you ever seen a car?"

The above depiction of Africa is very damaging to people who come to the U.S. from African countries. Many employers and others assume that we are uneducated and not competent enough to fill various jobs or positions in society. Furthermore, no one wants to be involved economically with different African countries because of the perception that it is a backward place. It's always amazing to me how people often call different European countries by name. People will speak of going to Germany, France and so on. But when many people go to African countries such as Kenya and Ethiopia, they often tend to say, "Over there in Africa . . ." To generalize Africa this way is like referring to Europe or Asia as a country.

When you say that you haven't seen real poverty until you went to Africa and don't specify a particular country, it would be like someone saying, "I never saw a drug-dealing, ignorant person until I met an African American." Of course such a statement is very ignorant and gives a wrong perception of African Americans. It is damaging to the African American community as a whole.

Margaret Akinay

I responded to Ms. Akinay with a sincere apology letter.

Dear Ms. Margaret Akinay:

First of all, I am so happy that you wrote me and that you are attending Bridgeway. I do hope that my comments, while they may have hurt you, do not at all reflect my heart on the matter *of Africa as a continent. Your correction was much needed and I receive it openly. Thank you so much for saying all that you said because I now know how my comments can be misconstrued. Although I know that Africa is a continent and not a country, I did not know how some Africans might be hurt by non-Africans like me speaking generally and not specifically about the continent. I clearly see now that the perceptions and stereotypes that can come from lumping the country and the continent together can have an adverse affect on the understanding of those who have not been to various African countries as I have.*

Thank you so much for clarifying and sharing this with me. I feel honored to have learned this from you and will seek to always be clear when I am speaking about Africa in general and certain countries in particular. Please accept my apology for making this error out of ignorance as to how I might be contributing to misperceptions of those from Africa. Will you please forgive me?

Pastor David

Ms. Akinay enlightened me on a specific way that I can be more considerate as to how the words I use affect her and others. When I speak about Africa, I now try to say "countries in Africa" or be even more specific about the actual country I'm referencing. In addition, whenever I speak about the poverty I experience there, I am careful to mention that I have met many educated people and wealthy people there as well, which is true. I do my best to make concerted efforts to include a fuller picture of the African continent amid so much media coverage about the need for assistance for the poorer populations within the various countries. Below is Ms. Akinay's response to my letter.

Dear Pastor Anderson,

Thank you very much for your reply to my letter. I felt a burden lifted from my heart when I read your letter. I have no problem at all in forgiving you and I ask that you may forgive me too if there was anything in my letter that came out as being rude. I know that you had very good intentions when you delivered that sermon, and that is why I do not hold anything against you. God has blessed you with a powerful, unique ministry and I feel blessed to be in Bridgeway. I will continue praying that God will continue to bless, encourage and strengthen you, and the church as a whole. Thank you again for your encouraging letter.

Margaret

"I will consider you" is not only a gracist saying but it also is a reality of living. Striving to do what we say makes our words come alive. Gracist living is about taking the sayings of Paul and living them out in the context of our lives and relationships. For me, considering others also means considering the words I use and the concepts I purport when preaching as it relates to other people groups and parts of the world. What does it mean for you?

REFLECTION QUESTIONS

1. Write in a journal about any encounters you have had with the homeless or poor. What were your initial thoughts and feelings? How do you normally respond to the homeless?

2. What reasons would the Levite and priest in the good Samaritan story give for avoiding the man on the side of the road? How are those reasons similar to your responses in question one?

3. What do you think the reasons were for the good Samaritan helping the man who was robbed?

4. How do you want God to minister through you to those who are in need? Can you identify ways that you might be able to position yourself to move in this direction?

10

SAYING SEVEN: "I WILL CELEBRATE WITH YOU"

(Rejoices with It)

If one part suffers, every part suffers with it;
if one part is honored, every part rejoices with it.

1 CORINTHIANS 12:26 (EMPHASIS ADDED)

At Bridgeway Community Church we try to circle around those who suffer. When a child dies, or a loved one leaves, our church family is swift at rallying around the hurting and those broken by grief. We will provide meals so those who grieve don't have to cook. We will arrange funerals, send pastors, organize prayer times, show up at memorial services and send flowers, cards and money to help ease the pain of the brokenhearted. When it comes to the homeless and the hungry, we clothe and feed them through our community cupboard and donations. While there is always more to do, I am grateful for the merciful, caring and generous hearts of our people. Many churches throughout the world reflect similar generosity. It is one of the greatest hallmarks of organized Christianity.

When others are hurting in the body, gracism demands that we sympathize with the pain of our brothers and sisters. When someone is unfairly or unjustly treated, we should stand with that person since we are all a part of one body.

I believe, however, that our church can develop more in the area of rejoicing, as is true for many Christians. Not simply rejoicing over what God has done in our personal lives, but the kind of rejoicing that Paul mentioned in 1 Corinthians 12:26, namely rejoicing with others over their successes. Just as you and I are to enter into the suffering and pain of others, so we are also to rejoice or celebrate with others.

When another racial group, ethnic group or gender group succeeds in some area, instead of becoming jealous or resentful, I should celebrate. This should be especially true when those who are downtrodden finally elevate. Imagine an unemployed person in your small-group Bible study weeping over his financial scarcity and the difficulty of finding another job. To make matters worse, this person doesn't have a degree; he quit his last job and has a pattern of not holding down employment due to some skill, attitude and personality issues. As a group you all pray for this person and do what you can to help.

How would you respond if this same person arrived at the Bible study the next week celebrating the fact that he was just hired by a large company that has agreed to pay him an annual six-figure salary with full benefits, stock options and an incentive program that would be a one-time payout of several hundred thousand dollars? Would you rejoice with him? Of course you would.

How about if you discovered that the position your group member was hired for was the same position that you applied for two months prior? You prayed for that position. You studied for the interview and hoped you would land the coveted opportunity. How would you respond now? It's a bit more difficult to rejoice now, right?

I believe Paul's heart in 1 Corinthians 12 is that there will be many different kinds of people in the Christian community. Some will have greater gifts than others. Some will have a different background educationally, racially or culturally. In all of this diversity we must rejoice with the successes of others, especially when it is not natural for us to rejoice in this way.

Do you think it is harder to rejoice with others or to suffer with them? Both can be difficult. Choosing to feel someone else's pain when I am not in pain can be challenging, but I think that rejoicing with others when I am desiring my own achievement can be even harder.

For example, look at the list of rejoicing below amid real circumstances of life. I am still called to rejoice with others when:

- someone in the body is having a baby, even though I am barren
- someone in the body gets a new car and I'm still walking
- someone in the body gets a new job or house and I'm struggling to achieve both

- someone in the body is getting married and I'm still single
- someone in the body receives applause for an achievement that I wish I had
- someone in the body had her child accepted into a college that my child didn't get into

Celebrating each other's successes and wins is critical to unity. Jealousy and covetousness brew the poison that brings dissension to the body.

I celebrate you when I encourage your success and acknowledge that you are doing well. I celebrate you when I call to offer congratulations or when I attend a party in your honor. Believe it or not, by celebrating others I am adding to the unity of the body and encouraging others in the body. Because rejoicing with others is not always easy, we need the Holy Spirit to help us.

When it comes to race relations, sometimes rejoicing can be even more difficult.

BLACK HISTORY MONTH CELEBRATIONS

The BridgeLeader Network is the consulting organization through which I train company executives on issues of multicultural leadership. In this role I have found that Black History Month produces tension within some companies. They have questions as to whether an entire month should be set aside to celebrate one group's heritage. While some whites and others argue that a month is too long, there are blacks who argue that it is the shortest month of the year. In addition a myriad of other issues flow from the debate. I usually land on the decision from a consultant's perspective that annual celebrations are nice but not necessary. However, the culture and atmosphere of the organization should help guide whether such a celebration is more for niceness or necessity.

I have told organizations not to call me to give speeches in February. If the company brings me in to speak on race relations during other months of the year, that demonstrates to me that they are serious about matters of diversity beyond an annual nod. Companies that are genuine in their celebration of Black History Month view the celebration as one of many different celebrations and do not view it simply as a token program to appease African Americans. I can usually sense the difference between the two perspectives. The token perspective is evident when the February celebration is the only program the company has and the only people interested in attending a celebration event are its organizers, along with a few guilty stragglers. The companies that are genuine in their diversity awareness have many celebrations throughout the year as they consistently elevate the value of celebration. They observe other culturally significant dates throughout the year as well. Celebrations beyond traditional ones like Christmas and Independence Day include the following: Juneteenth, the celebration on June 19 to commemorate the abolition of slavery; St. Patrick's Day; Asian Pacific Heritage Month; Kwanzaa; Yom Kippur; Ramadan; Dr. Martin Luther King Jr.'s birthday; and Cinco de Mayo, the legendary Mexican holiday on the fifth of May.

I have been to companies that have committees, leadership teams and boards that focus solely on developing and maintaining a culture of celebration and acceptance. In a multicultural country like ours it is very important to honor and rejoice with others who find significance in their upbringing and backgrounds.

For churches, cultural celebrations can be tricky because celebrating Jesus Christ is where we as Christians find our greatest joy and commonality. Believers in Jesus never want to feel as though they are compromising their doctrinal purity for social or political correctness. Therefore a rule of thumb that may help churches is to engage only in those cultural celebrations that do not contradict the values of the Christian faith. Other than that, the sky is the limit as long as the church keeps Christ at the core.

When our church hosts international food festivals and multicultural dinners, we have exposed our people to the richness of other cultures that they may not have experienced before. They taste foods, hear music and learn aspects of people's lives that they would not have known simply by sitting next to someone from another culture in church.

Last year at our staff Christmas party we highlighted a multicultural cuisine that included two Korean soup dishes, an African American entrée (a.k.a. soul food), Puerto Rican and West African side dishes followed by a European custard dessert. Our icebreaker was a cultural proficiency game in which staff members had to answer humorous questions in order to receive prizes throughout the night. The party was hosted at the large home of a Puerto Rican staff member. After the dinner the tables were removed so we could dance. We were taught some salsa dance moves. Some of us learned more quickly than others. Some of us never learned. All of us had fun.

I'm also reminded of a Valentine's Day dinner Bridgeway hosted where professional ballroom dancers taught couples how to square dance. For many this was indeed a cultural experience. Celebrating in different ways, employing many different cultural ideas, is a fun way to do life together. Each year several of our members join for a Passover Seder in which they share in a Jewish meal to remember the cultural and spiritual lineage of Christ. Through various multicultural expressions we experience God in ways that we would not otherwise have the privilege of doing. Rejoicing with others can be quite entertaining.

MULTICULTURAL VOICE BOXES

Out of the nine speakers who teach from the platform on Sundays there is a diversity of styles in communication. From a prophetic preaching style to a didactic teaching style to a comedic conversational style, Bridgeway tries to consistently feed the body good soul food. I'm sure there are times when we do not hit the mark, but we try. Five of our communicators are white (four men and one woman), and four of the speakers are men of color (two black, one Korean and one Latino). When the Holy Spirit choreographs unity at our church, he coordinates preferences and styles, cultures, races and genders as well. It is beautiful to watch God combine the parts of his body just as he imagined. By having a Korean preacher give the Word, Koreans are honored. Having a Filipino on stage to act out a lead role in a drama sketch communicates to Filipinos and other Asians that they have a stake in this ministry. When a Puerto Rican preaches, Latinos rejoice. When a woman teaches, half our population is lifted high. We believe that our culturally diverse population is celebrated by representation.

Minority representation brings a sense of rejoicing to minority populations that the majority may sometimes overlook. Celebrating achievement, access and the elevation of other groups is a practical way to enter into the joy of others.

Regardless of race or gender, when one adds the distinctions of diversity to the mouthpieces of the church, it broadens the styles and perspectives of God's Word being taught to his blended body. God clearly speaks through different voice boxes. Those men and women whom he speaks through come in different colors and from different cultures.

MULTICULTURAL WORSHIP

Hearing the Word of God through multicultural voice boxes is one thing, but celebrating in worship together with people from dozens of nations is breathtaking. The ultimate celebration of Christians is not the celebration of each other's culture but rather occurs when all of those cultures unite at the foot of the cross and sing at the top of their lungs, "Shout to the Lord, all the earth, let us sing." When from the depths of our hearts we sing in unison, "Great is thy faithfulness." Worshiping God together is the most awesome celebration of all. I can't imagine what it must feel like to God, and look like to the angels, to witness a multicultural legion of worshipers lifting up the name of Jesus as Lord and King from the bottom of their hearts.

It is out of this kind of worship that we honor one another. As one body joined under one head, Jesus Christ, and out of our commitment to Christ and love for one another, we rejoice with those who rejoice.

Can you say, "I will celebrate with you" to others in your church? Whether it is someone in your small group who lands a new job, a woman who has a new baby, someone who has been blessed financially or a racial group that achieves a significant social milestone? Saying "I will celebrate with you" adds to the unity of the church and counteracts resentment, bitterness, jealousy and covetousness.

MISSING PIECE

I love Paul's summary statement that puts a stake in the ground and exclaims, "Now you are the body of Christ, and each one of you is a part of it" (1 Corinthians 12:27). That says it all, doesn't it?

We are all a part of God's kingdom puzzle. Each piece of a puzzle is essential. Have you ever put a puzzle together and discovered that one or two pieces were missing? I put together a one-hundred-piece puzzle with my son last spring and we had ninety-nine pieces. That one missing piece drove us crazy! Finally, after searching in every possible place, we found that one little piece on the floor. Ah, now we were able to rest because the puzzle was complete. Whether the puzzle piece is big or small, an inside or a corner piece, a colorful or a monochrome piece, it is essential to completing the picture of the puzzle.

Last year I gave each of my staff members a puzzle-shaped pin they could wear to signify that each of us is an important piece of the body of Christ in general and an essential piece of the Bridgeway Community Church puzzle in particular. The message is a simple one—we are linked as one and we need each other.

Likewise Paul declared that we are all a part of God's kingdom puzzle and that everyone in your community of believers is a part of it too. The church down the street is a puzzle piece, as is the one on the other side of town. There is no part of the body, no piece of the puzzle that is expendable or dispensable. Therefore let us refuse to treat anyone as if he or she doesn't matter. Each person's perspective, gifts, history and experiences matter to God and should matter to us.

WHITE PIECES

As it relates to racial reconciliation, whites must have a place where they can voice their fears and ideas as well. They are a piece of God's diversity puzzle and should not be squeezed out of the celebration of multicultural unity. When I was teaching a cultural diversity course to working adults seeking their college degrees at the University of Phoenix, I asked my class if they wanted to read one of the letters from the manuscript of a book I was writing at the time, *Letters Across the Divide*. This book was a compilation of letters between a white business-man, Brent Zuercher, and me, a black pastor. For three years, from Chicago to Maryland, Brent and I dealt honestly with is-sues of race in our relationship via letters. Brent's questions to me, such as "Why is everything a racial issues for blacks?" "Why do I have to call you African American?" and "Who should apologize?" were the types of questions we discussed and debated. One evening in class we read the letter dealing with the question "Why are blacks so angry?" A white woman, Dana, read Brent's letter addressed to me, and then Tina, a black woman, was assigned to read my response to Brent aloud, after which the class was to have an open discussion about what was read.

After Dana read Brent's letter to me in front of the class, an interesting twist of emotion took place. Brent's letter stated something to the effect of "I'm sick and tired of black preachers fanning flames of hate from their pulpits, and I'm exhausted by blacks crying wolf and whining about racism all the time. Love, Brent."

When Dana had finished reading this, the multicultural class of fifteen adults was silent. You could hear a pin drop in the room. Before moving on I acknowledged the awkwardness and asked the class what they were feeling. The woman who had just read Brent's letter began to shake. Her face began to flush red as tears welled up in her eyes and began to stream down her cheeks. "Dana," I said, "what's making you emotional?"

She responded in a stuttering fashion, as if to catch her breath from crying, "This is the way I feel."

Dana was a champion for diversity in her company and never saw herself as culturally incompetent. However, she never had her deeper thoughts expressed, validated or even elevated to a question. She didn't know that anyone could actually express thoughts out loud like Brent did and not immediately be carted off as a racist. Brent was able to write these letters because of the safety of our friendship. Many whites don't have a venue where they can test their thoughts, ask their questions, communicate their objections or voice their frustrations. Without such a forum learning will not take place and comprehension will be aborted by a stronger resolve to resist change. In the forum of this classroom a safe place had been established, and Dana recognized through it that she had deeper unspoken feelings that Brent was unearthing.

The most beautiful thing was what happened next. Tina, the African American woman assigned to read my letter of response to Brent, set down her papers, walked over to Dana and hugged the white woman tightly. As they held each other, crying, the entire secular classroom became emotional. What a beautiful snapshot of reconciliation! A black woman and a white woman hugging as a way of communicating hurt, forgiveness, pain, comfort, understanding and acceptance was a moment to remember. It was a special moment for our class. The barriers were down and real conversation erupted. No one was muted. The white experience was a puzzle piece that couldn't be left on the floor. As a gracist I must let whites know that they are a part of the multicultural body of Christ, lest they think that multicultural means everyone else but them. Every piece of the puzzle matters.

UNEARTHING YOUR DIVERSITY STORY

Everyone has a diversity story. Whether white, black, brown, red or yellow, we all have a story. To unearth it, questions like the following are good discussion starters:

- "When did you realize that you were different from others?"
- "When did you realize there was a race problem in society?"
- "How has growing up with no diversity affected your view of diverse people?"

One of the ways of communicating to others that they matter to us is listening to their stories. Opening the door to multicultural dialogue provides space for storytelling. This can be done in small groups, during Bible studies or even at multicultural fellowship dinners hosted between churches. All that is needed is a vision and a desire to have such a gathering with an open Bible, an open mind and hearts that are open to listen and love. The Holy Spirit delights in guiding these kinds of gatherings in order to reveal God's bigger story of redemption and reconciliation. He wants to help us to be answers to Jesus' prayer for unity, one puzzle piece at a time.

REFLECTION QUESTIONS

1. Can you remember a time when it was difficult for you to rejoice with someone else? Share why it was hard.

2. While growing up, when did you realize that you were different from others? How are you still different? How does being different make you feel?

3. How do you view whites in the diversity conversation? If you are a white person, do you feel like you have a voice? Explain. If you are a nonwhite person, do you feel like whites have something to offer when it comes to diversity? Why or why not?

11

How Can I Become a Gracist?

In this book you have read that everyone has dots. We all have issues, experiences, gifts and distinctions that must be integrated into the puzzle of the kingdom life. How do people from different backgrounds live together in unity within the body of Christ? How do we live out our faith beyond the walls of the body of Christ as parts of the broader human family? I have highlighted seven sayings from Paul's words in 1 Corinthians that you can cling to as you struggle with what it means to be a reconciler in a divided world and church. Here are the sayings once again from 1 Corinthians 12:22-26:

1. "I will lift you up" (special honor, verse 23).

2. "I will cover you" (special modesty, verse 23).

3. "I will share with you" (no special treatment, verse 24).

4. "I will honor you" (greater honor, verse 24).

5. "I will stand with you" (no division, verse 25).

6. "I will consider you" (equal concern, verse 25).

7. "I will celebrate with you" (rejoices with it, verse 26).

Imagine saying these phrases to your spouse, pastor, church leadership team, small group, family members or a racial group that God lays on your heart. It is a powerful thing to say these phrases with a deep sense of personal commitment.

SPIRIT-LED COMMUNITY

Beyond individual commitments there is a communal commitment that brings all we have stated full circle. Paul spoke of the individual parts of the body as an interconnected and interlinked unit. These sayings, lived out in community through small groups, covenant groups and support groups, bring to us the mutuality of interdependence that lifts us up as one. Christian community is essential to body life and is the container within which the Holy Spirit delights in moving.

In 1 Corinthians 12:4-6 Paul precedes the human body illustration with the leadership of the Holy Spirit. This is one of only two times in the New Testament where the Holy Spirit is mentioned in the first position when referring to the triune God. Notice the text: "There are different kinds of gifts, but the same *Spirit*. There are different kinds of service, but the same *Lord*. There are different kinds of working, but the same *God* works all of them in all men" (emphasis added). The only other place in the New Testament where the third person of the Trinity is placed first is in Ephesians 4:4-6: "There is one body and one *Spirit*—just as you were called to one hope when you were called—one *Lord*, one faith, one baptism; one *God* and Father of all, who is over all and through all and in all" (emphasis added).

Don't you find it interesting that in both places in Scripture the context of the Spirit's leadership is oneness? Both passages are speaking to the issue of unity through diversity. I truly believe that the unity of the body is a spiritual matter first and foremost. God's Spirit delights in breaking down barriers and adjoining different parts of the body—causing them to dance. The Holy Spirit is the breath within the body that gives life to all the parts. Even when Jesus prayed for the oneness of the church, as recorded in John 17, he did so after the discourse of the Holy Spirit recorded in John 16. The Acts 2 passage that outlines the inauguration of the New Testament church is set off by the movement of the Holy Spirit among the diverse crowd of new believers.

My point is that it takes the movement of the Holy Spirit to work among the individual members, revealing to them their desperate need for one another. It seems to me that the Spirit's job is to move within a community, aligning, ordering and interconnecting various parts of the body to ease their working together like oil moving within an engine or machine. When Spirit-led believers come together in communal interdependence, the Spirit maximizes kingdom potential and moves in dynamic and unpredictable ways. When believers come together in prayer and unity, the Spirit is invited to act.

I am reminded of the story of the dry bones in Ezekiel 37. God, in a dream, instructed Ezekiel to preach to a valley of dry bones, representing the need for the restoration of Israel. The breath and movement of the Spirit came after the bones in the valley were organized and put together. Preceding the organization of the bones in the valley was the prophetic preaching of Ezekiel. My hope is that this book, along with the messages of others who have been called to write and preach this message, will be a prophetic call for the church, like that addressed to the dry bones, to come together. When we move in that direction, the Spirit will lift the church to levels unseen in our divided world and churches.

As I stated earlier in the book, gracism is the positive extension of favor on other humans based on color, class or culture. Racism can be narrow in its definition. Grace is the opposite, though. It is wide and all encompassing. In many ways race and class are on ramps to the broader highway of grace for many people if we choose to use it this way. Instead of using race, class and culture as negative descriptors that cause us to resist one another, I am challenging us to use these distinctives as opportunities to extend grace more fully—gracism. I would add that this extension of favor must include all who are on the fringes regardless of their gifts, abilities or distinctions. It is the call and responsibility of the majority to extend grace to the minority in all cases. By becoming a gracist, you will be more like Christ and will become a bridge builder for unity. Will you say yes to this call?

Below are some practical suggestions of what you can do to begin your gracist journey of reconciliation.

1. RECEIVE THE GRACE OF GOD IN YOUR LIFE FIRST

The Bible is clear that we have all sinned and have fallen way short of reaching God's standard of perfection (Romans 3:23). Our sinful condition causes all of us to be separated from God (death) and forever lost in our waywardness (Romans 6:23). Because of his grace God has purposefully reached out to build a bridge to the human race and has offered salvation from eternal separation and forgiveness of sin. Such love can come only from God. He loves you and me so much that he extends his gracious hand toward each of us (John 3:16). All we have to do is accept his unbelievable proposal.

If you have not given your RSVP to God's loving proposal to forgive you for your sin and begin a personal relationship of trust with him, then now is the time for you to respond to God. Pause right now, close your eyes and picture God on one knee extending to you his divine hand of proposal. Will you pray and say to God, "I do"? Tell him that you accept his proposal to forgive you and walk with you forever in a relationship. Ask God to forgive you. Ask him to come into your life and be your Lord and Savior. Pray in faith and believe that you are forgiven and cleansed. God promises to respond to your cry and hear your prayer even now (Romans 10:13).

You may want to say a prayer to God like the one below or a similar one using your own words:

Dear God, I know that I am a sinner who is separated from you. I know that I need a Savior, and Jesus Christ, you are him. I invite you into my life today to be my Lord and Savior. Please forgive me for my sin. I choose to follow you by faith today. I

believe in you. I accept your divine proposal to forgive me and
walk with me forever. I give my life to you now. In Jesus' name,
amen.

If you prayed the above prayer with a sincere heart, the Bible promises that you are saved (Romans 10:9-10, 13). The next step for you is to find a church family or a community of believers who can help you grow in your faith. If you have a Christian friend or family member, contact that person and tell him or her about what you just prayed. It will encourage that person and hopefully she or he will be able to help you along the way in your faith. Feel free to e-mail me personally through my website at <www.BridgewayOnline.org> and let me know that you prayed this prayer. I will do my best to help you find a church or get some material in your hands to help you in your journey. I want to hear from you.

If you have already received Christ as your Lord and Savior, then you are a personal example and recipient of God's grace. Are you now ready to extend it to others?

2. REACH OVER THE COLOR LINE BY INVITING SOMEONE TO YOUR CHURCH OR HOME

If you are a Christian, let me encourage you to invite someone who is on the other side of the racial, ethnic or economic divide to your church, small group or home this month. Please don't do this for my sake, but do it for God's sake. This is what the body of Christ is to be. God's children are from every color, class and culture. For example, if you are black, I encourage you to invite a white or Hispanic person to your church or home. If you are white, invite a black person to your church or home. If you are Vietnamese, why not invite a non-Asian over for dinner? If you are Puerto Rican, reach out to a Mexican and build a friendship. This is where concept and reality intersect from theory to practical life.

Christianity at its best is a faith that reaches across lines of comfort and convenience (Acts 1:8). It is a faith that follows the model of its founder, Jesus Christ, who gave up the prerogatives of his divine nature and became a humble and obedient servant as a man (Philippians 2:6-8). He did this not for a one-time dinner date but for an everlasting relationship. Maybe a small-group atmosphere where you can mix with people from other backgrounds will help you become comfortable with others as a step toward spending alone time with them over coffee or dinner. Is there a family in your Sunday school class, Bible study meeting or weekly fellowship group whom you might be able to engage in conversation? Why not begin there and see what God does through your faith? He desires for gracism to work more than we do. I promise that he will come through.

3. READ ON THE SUBJECT OF RECONCILIATION

Another way to grow as a new gracist is to read on subjects that help you understand the culture, plight and history of other ethnic and racial groups. I have found that most bridge builders are people who are learners and not know-it-alls. It takes great effort to read and learn about other people whom you have no need to know in order to survive or succeed. Electing to do so is an act of love and will speak volumes to those about whom you learn.

I commend my previous books, *Letters Across the Divide* (Baker, 2001) and *Multicultural Ministry* (Zondervan, 2004), to you. I hope you will read these if you have not done so already; they will help you build racial bridges in life and ministry. While this may sound a bit self-promotional, my heart has vested much into these works, and I believe they will serve you well. In addition many others have invested their lives, ministries and intellects into reconciliation, Christian unity and aspects of multicultural ministry that can be extremely helpful to learners as well. Please see my reading list at the end of the book.

4. RELATE ON PURPOSE TO PEOPLE WHO ARE DIFFERENT

Make it your business to shop, work out, eat or play in parts of town where you have a higher probability of interacting with people who are different from you. I know this may seem far-fetched and out of the way, but think of how far Christ came to build a relationship with us on earth. Think how Jesus purposed to walk through Samaria to meet the Samaritan woman at the well. If we don't purpose to relate to others whom we can easily ignore, we will miss the blessings of gracism. In so doing we will reap the wonderful learning that comes when we reach out. Namely, that we ourselves have been reached and blessed in ways we never knew. When we seek to include, we discover that the very ones we reached out to have something we are missing. There is a piece of God that we lack when we exclude others who reflect something of him that we could not in any other way see.

5. Link with a Church or Organization That Promotes Care for the Poor

It is imperative that we join hands with others who seek to relieve oppression, racism, poverty and hunger. Our Lord clearly illustrates that his followers are to demonstrate love and goodness to those less fortunate (Matthew 25:40). Do a Web search for a ministry or nonprofit entity that you can support in your local area or around the world to be a part of the solution to suffering.

A Closing Word

I end this book with an African proverb that has guided me in bridge building and racial healing. While I still have a long way to go, this proverb reminds me that dialogue begins the process of relating and respecting those who are different than me.

When I saw him from afar, I thought he was a monster.
When he got closer, I thought he was just an animal.
When he got closer, I recognized that he was a human.
When we were face to face, I realized that he was
      my brother.

As long as we keep people at a distance, we can categorize

them as monsters or animals. But when we get closer and begin to communicate with each other, we recognize that people are just like us in many ways. Comprehension begins with conversation. Essential to grace is a person who is willing to receive it and then out of a grace-filled heart is compelled to extend it. May God bless you and keep you as you embrace, exemplify and educate others about gracism.

Reading List

Anderson, David. *Multicultural Ministry*. Grand Rapids: Zondervan, 2004.

Anderson, David, and Brent Zuercher. *Letters Across the Divide*. Grand Rapids: Baker, 2001.

DeYoung, Curtiss Paul, Michael O. Emerson, George Yancey and Karen Chai Kim. *United by Faith*. New York: Oxford University Press, 2003.

Emerson, Michael O., and Christian Smith. *Divided by Faith*. Oxford: Oxford University Press, 2000.

Evans, Anthony. *Let's Get to Know Each Other*. Nashville: Thomas Nelson, 1995.

Goode, Wilson. *In Goode Faith*. Elgin, Ill.: Judson Press, 1994.

Law, Eric H. F. *Inclusion: Making Room for Grace*. St. Louis: Chalice Press, 2000.

Myrdal, Gunnar. *The American Dilemma*. New York: Harper, 1944.

Pannell, William. *The Coming Race War*. Grand Rapids: Zondervan, 1993.

Peart, Norman Anthony. *Separate No More*. Grand Rapids: Baker, 2000.

Perkins, John, and Thomas A. Tarrants III. *He's My Brother.* Grand Rapids: Chosen Books, 1994.

Perkins, Matali. "Guess Who's Coming to Church?" *Christianity Today*, March 7, 1994.

Perkins, Spencer, and Chris Rice. *More Than Equals*. Downers Grove, Ill.: InterVarsity Press, 1993.

Perry, Dwight. *Breaking Down Barriers*. Grand Rapids: Baker, 1998.

Rossman, Marlene L. *Multicultural Marketing*. New York: Amacom, 1994.

Schaeffer, Francis A. *The Church at the End of the Twentieth Century*. Downers Grove, Ill.: InterVarsity Press, 1970.

Skinner, Barbara Williams. "Been There, Done That." *The Reconciler* (winter 1996).

Sniffen, Michael J. *FBI: Hate Crimes Motivated by Race*. Associated Press, February 13, 2001.

Stewart, John. *Bridges Not Walls*. New York: McGraw Hill, 1995.

Thernston, Stephan, and Abigail Thernston. *America in Black and White*. New York: Simon & Schuster, 1997.

Washington, Raleigh, and Glen Kehrein. *Breaking Down Walls*. Chicago: Moody Press, 1993.

West, Cornel. *Prophesy Deliverance!* Philadelphia: Westminster Press, 1982.

_____. *Race Matters*. Boston: Beacon Press, 1993.

Woodson, Carter G. *The History of the Negro Church*. Third edition. Washington, D.C.: Associated Publishers, 1992.

Yancey, George. *Beyond Racial Gridlock*. Downers Grove, Ill.: InterVarsity Press, 2006.

NOTES

Introduction

page 11   gracism, unlike racism: David A. Anderson, *Multicultural Ministry* (Grand Rapids: Zondervan, 2004).

Chapter 2: From Racism to Gracism

page 21   I define racism: David A. Anderson, *Letters Across the Divide* (Grand Rapids: Baker, 2001).

page 21   I define gracism: David A. Anderson, *Multicultural Ministry* (Grand Rapids: Zondervan, 2004).

Chapter 3: The Art of Inclusion

page 31   almost 50 percent: Richard D. Bucher, *Diversity Consciousness* (Upper Saddle River, N.J.: Prentice-Hall, 2000).

page 31   Three out of ten people: Jordan T. Pine, *Accurate Census Count of Minorities,* DiversityInc.com, February 14, 2001.

page 32   At the current rate: Marlene L. Rossman, *Multicultural Marketing* (New York: Amacom, 1994).

Chapter 7: Saying Four: "I Will Honor You" (Greater Honor)

page 97   After his stint: Wilson Goode, *In Goode Faith* (Elgin, Ill.: Judson Press, 1994).

ABOUT THE AUTHOR

David Anderson is the founder and senior pastor of Bridge-way Community Church, a multicultural congregation located in Columbia, Maryland. He is also the founder and president of the BridgeLeader Network (www.bridgeleader.com), a multicultural leadership consulting organization, and an instructor of cultural diversity at the University of Phoenix, Maryland campuses. Dr. Anderson received his bachelor's and master's degrees from Moody Bible Institute and his doctor of philosophy degree in the sociological integration of religion and society at Oxford Graduate School. He has coauthored a book titled *Letters Across the Divide: Two Friends Explore Racism, Friendship and Faith* (2001), which has generated media interest nationwide through exposure on over two thousand radio stations and television appearances, which include Black Entertainment Television (BET), CSPAN, TBN, PAX and ABC, promoting his message of diversity. Dr. Anderson hosts a live radio show, called *Reconciliation Live* (www.reconciliationlive.com), on the largest Christian radio station in Washington, D.C. (WAVA

105.1FM), and is syndicated to forty-eight states and three countries through XM 170 satellite radio. His second book, *Multicultural Ministry: Finding Your Church's Unique Rhythm* (2004), highlights his messages and lessons in doing multicultural ministry. Dr. Anderson is a highly sought after conference speaker, lecturer and consultant on local, national and international levels. Dr. Anderson is married and has three young children who make their home in Maryland.

ABOUT BRIDGEWAY COMMUNITY CHURCH

Founded by David and Amber Anderson in the spring of 1992 with a handful of others, Bridgeway Community Church, a multicultural, nondenominational, performing arts church was born. Bridgeway is located in Columbia, Maryland, and exceeds two thousand people in weekly attendance from racially and culturally diverse backgrounds (www.bridgewayonline.org).

BridgeLeader
B O O K S

ABOUT BRIDGELEADER BOOKS

BridgeLeader Books are produced through a partnership between InterVarsity Press and BridgeLeader Network, a nonprofit organization that helps churches, colleges, companies and other groups move toward multicultural effectiveness. Addressing such topics as reconciliation, diversity and leadership development, BridgeLeader Books contribute to a better understanding and practice of multicultural ministry within the church and in the world.